MW00678354

I hope this inspires you to PERSUE your dreams

[signature] (K.D.)

ABOUT THE AUTHOR

I started writing poetry back in 2009. I was inspired by my older sister Miriam who also wrote poetry so I figured it was in my "DANA"(D.N.A) also to write. My first attempt was a book called OBKNOXIOUSLY YOURS TRULY Poems of Life I illustrated the cover for, wrote and had printed in six months to see if I could do it. Since then I have been writing and collecting poems. These are 120 of the more "palatable" ones I have written over the last ten years that might keep me off of the "No Fly List" and out of an asylum. If some of my poetry's themes seem to reiterate themselves, it's only because life itself is reiterating.

K.D. KNOX

PEN ART

Poems of Life

KENNETH D. KNOX

All rights reserved. No part of this book may be reproduced or transmitted in any form or by any means, electronic or mechanical, including photocopying, recording, or by any information storage and retrieval system without the written permission of the author, except where permitted by law.

©2020KDKNOX

ISBN (Print Edition): 978-1-09833-740-7

ISBN (eBook Edition): 978-1-09833-741-4

Printed in the United States

First Edition

Acknowledgements

Chawn " Mr. Magic "Paige----Computer Tech Advisor

Angela "Tweedle" Tyson----Photography

Dedications

To my three children Karin, Majul and Keenan. My seven grandkids, The Knox Klan and all of my friends that inspired me and "pushed my pen" to create these eclectic writings over the last ten years.

Table of Contents

Pen Art

If I could write a Rembrandt

What words would I choose

If I could pen a Picasso

Which pens would I use

To portray such beauty

Of purple, rose and gold

Into expressive words

For the mind's eyes to behold

Words that stir imagination

And make emotions flare

To make you feel weightless

Like floating on thin air

How can I write the ruby reds

And the ice-cool blues

Mixed with the emerald greens

With a hint of yellowish hues

A giant reddish-orange sun

Setting into a blue ocean

Behind a sailboat clipping the water

In an easy, effortless motion

How can I wield my pen

Like an extension of my eyes

To make you feel a breeze

Under the clear blue skies

With words from my soul

Flowing to the tip of my pen

Arriving spiritually painted

Written from deep within

If I could write a Rembrandt

It would be words from my heart

To bring color to the world

By sharing my pen's art

At The Day's End

At the end of the day when the dust settles

Did you make someone smile

Or leave someone alone and sad

Did you sleep with a song in your heart

Or toss and turn angry and mad

At the end of the day when the dust settles

Did you have a wonderful day

Getting things done

In a productive way

Or did all your plans go sour

With grief hour to hour

Now you are probably thinking

If I had more money

My life wouldn't be as funny

Bad outcomes come from poor incomes

It's hard to produce good outcomes

From bad incomes

But money doesn't make you happy

While a lack thereof makes you sad

Learn to live in the happy medium

Between the two

Whereas a little of both

Will suffice and do

The outcome that will be

Derive from the dreams you foresee

Think it twice and do it once

For a better outcome and response

COGITO ERGO SUM

(I think therefore I am)

Lucatyounow!!!

(Pronounced "LOOK AT YOU NOW"
Pacino style from *Scarface*)

If I show you the good in me

Then tell you the bad in me

What do you see???

If I shared my innermost feelings

Then you saw my wheelings and dealings

Did you see what you wanted to see

Or who you thought I should be

Most people have something to hide

When revealing scars from inside

Buried deep by errors and trials

Covered up by years of denials

Lurking behind the curtain of the wizard

Could be a man eating lizard

Or a cute little kitten

Playing with your lost mitten

What we see in others

Is based on expectations of our own

To reshape another as we see

Into a mirrored flawless clone

When unexpected results

Produce an unexplained reality

Then you have a problem digesting

Who you see as me

Why can't you see

That regardless of what you see

You are still just like me

Whether a religious wrongdoing sinner

Or an agnostic good-doing saint

You ain't what you see you are

And you might be what you see you ain't

The Eyes Of A Child

If we could travel back in time

To be a child for one day

Live without a care in the world

With all day long to play

To lie in a field of flowers

Staring blankly into space

While imagining we are on Mars

Or some other faraway place

We could turn clouds in the sky

Into fire-breathing dragons

Imagine driving race cars

While sitting in our wagons

Envision Santa and Rudolph

Perched upon our roof

Believe that the Tooth Fairy

Brought us money for a tooth

Children view this world through innocent eyes

With its faults all mired in sin

They have yet to experience life

As a game to lose or win

A child sees only people

There is no black or white

Until they are taught by someone

To alter and ruin their sight

A child should stay a child

As long as they possibly can

They should not bypass their youth

And rush from a boy into a man

Once they have grown up

To become worldly and wise

They will no longer see this world

Through their innocent child eyes

If we could travel back in time

To live one day as a child

We need to bring back their innocent eyes

To make our present days worthwhile

The Closet Tailor

There is someone in my closet

I know this might sound a little strange

But when I hang my clothes in there

They always seem to change

There must be a tailor in there

Altering my large shirts to small

Cause sometimes when I take them out to wear

I cannot get into them at all

And when I hang my pants in there

They suddenly appear to shrink

There is someone in my closet

And it's not what you think

The length of my pants never change

They always change the waist

Maybe the closet tailor does this

To create more closet space

They make the shirt buttons stress

And the pants tight around the thigh

I fear the belt and buttons might fly loose

And pop someone in the eye

Though all of my clothes are shrinking

I still have some good news

One thing they could not do

Is shrink my tennis shoes

To trick the tailor in my closet

I finally figured out what to do

Instead of hanging up pants size 38

I will hang up size 42

Confused And Black

Kidnapped, addled, confused and black

Fettered and flogged on our back

Totally against our desires and will

With deep scars that may never heal

Across miles of a shark-infested ocean

To a place of which we had no notion

To pick cotton and work the land

Upon our slave master's demand

We were given our master's last name

For him to stake his undue claim

Of everything that we did own

Right down to our women's moan

What makes a man's heart so cruel

To make another man his tool

What makes a man's heart so cold

To deny another the privilege of growing old

Against the odds we have survived

Over time our generations have thrived

Now unfettered and unchained

What have we realized and gained

Prisoners now in our own skin

Not remembering where we've been

Still plagued by our mental scars

In wet cold cells with iron bars

With children born out of wedlock

Drug dealing on the neighborhood block

Without taking lessons from the past

How long will this false freedom last

While time is wearily wearing thin

Some are still right where we began

Still some survival skills we lack

Some still addled, confused and black

Rap On Brother

What is going on with all of these wannabe rap stars

Sitting and sipping drinks in their neighborhood bars

Do they really think they have a shot at the big times

Just because once they spit out a few good rhymes

You will see them at most of the latest clubs

Still rolling with paper license tags on doves

Usually riding in an old Chevy or Olds

Newly painted with dents in both of the doors

In the club they can only make it rain with pennies

A night on the town consists of eating at Denny's

They might have a job at the Burger King

So that they can pay for their tattoos and bling

They probably never even finished high school

Convinced that school is made for a fool

Still living at home with their sister and mother

Cause their paychecks won't take them any further

Just waiting on their rap contract to come through

So they can finally get what they are due

They probably will never make the big show

To get fame, fine cars and lots of dough

Some people will never reach the big time

Because it is a long uphill climb

It is improbable for everyone to think they can be

A rap star like Snoop or Jay Z

If they want to know the real deal

It is best to start out with schooling or a skill

Then if your rap star vision suddenly goes south

You can still put some food in your mouth

Hyde's Pride

It's hard for people to keep

An even composure every day

Most have a tendency to flip-flop

Depending on obstacles in their way

They mostly want to stay happy

With joy and warmth to cast

But sometimes they get troubled

Burdened with cavils of their past

Then out comes your Mr. Hyde

In goes your Dr. Jekyll

Making your current situation

Just one big nasty pickle

It is only human nature

To have a Jekyll and a Hyde

Their only mitigating control

Seems to be one's humanly pride

Pride appears to be

A very remarkable feature

That keeps our Hyde calmly at bay

Encaging our innermost creature

Pride also serves as

The mind's most useful tool

To keep our family and friends

From seeing us act a fool

Most of the things we think bad

Do not deserve an action

Let your pride take over

To steer you in the right direction

While unleashing your Dr. Jekyll

And stifling your Mr. Hyde

To calm your raging seas

With a hefty dose of pride

My Brother, My Brother

I am the tenth out of eleven children

Born to Nazareth and Lessie Knox

We all inherited very good genes

That made us as clever as a fox

We all have a very acute perception

We all know when to come out of the rain

We all know when it is time to fold

When there is nothing else to gain

I have lived to be sixty plus years old

While enjoying a marginal wealth and fame

But I still have an older brother

That cannot even remember my name

Most of the time he calls me by

The name of my other brother

I guess at least he got it half right

Because we do have the same mother

Often I just reply to it

I don't want to get him off track

Then sometimes I wonder to myself

Did he run out of crack???

I used to think he was joking

Then I learned that he really wasn't

At least he did call me by my brother's name

Instead of a distant cousin

My older brother is extremely smart

With the I.Q. of a genius

He even taught me when I was young

It's not a wee-wee, It's a penis

I'm not going to call your name out

Because you know who you are

So just do me one big favor

And don't ever ask to borrow my car

You might return it to my brother

Or some other faraway place

Then it will be lost just like me

Without a name or a trace

My Dreams

My dreams are an array of many colors

For my slumbering eyes to behold

They are very real and vivid spectrums

Of red, blue, green, purple and gold

My dreams are usually peaceful and simple

Sometimes dangerous and complicated

They often occur in the weirdest places

Where a sense of time is overrated

In my dreams there are many people

Some young, some old, some I don't know

Some of these people are still living

Some have passed away long ago

At times I see some childhood buddies

Whose lives were cut short by chance

That never knew the joys and woes

Of living, fatherhood and romance

Out of all of the people in my dreams

I enjoy seeing my mom and dad

Knowing that they are finally at rest

And the wonderful life they had

My parents lived a blessed full life

And peacefully passed away

Still in my dreams they are much alive

As real as a bright sunny day

They are always cheerful and happy

With auras lit by the sun's beams

Though I'll never again see them while awake

I will see them in my dreams

The Privilege

When I was younger I used to hear old folks say

How it used to be and what they used to do

As a naïve young man I thought these sayings were dumb

I grew weary listening to tales from old folks of

How it used to be and what they used to do

As a young man who "knew" everything

I always thought they were dumb also

Out of touch with the real world

Little then did I know that

If I cheated death and side-stepped health issues

I would become one of these old folks

With memories of what I used to do

As my late great mother used to say

"Don't frown upon getting old

Because many are denied the privilege"

Being young and thinking I would live forever

I never gave her saying much thought until

I noticed many of the friends I grew up with

Being denied that privilege

As a youth, sex and drugs were the order of the day

No one put much stock into getting old

Growing old gracefully was a myth

Not in the grasp of the mind of a young fool

Who "knew" everything

Growing old gracefully is still a myth

Most do not grow old gracefully

Most grow old moaning, aching

While kicking and screaming

Like a lil B........(baby)

As the old saying goes which is true

"Youth is wasted on the young"

I thank God for growing older and wiser

To have "The Privilege" to write

These words being for now in good health

While enjoying retirement with

A "reasonably" sound state of mind

Drilling For Dinosaurs

Here fossil fuel, Here fossil fuel

Just where can you be?

We drill for you on dry land

And underneath the sea

They say you come from dinosaurs

Long gone in the past

If we keep drilling for you

This poor earth will not last

It might not be tomorrow

But soon we will have to pay

For what we have done to the earth

As of yesterday and today

If God really wanted his earth

To be barren and full of holes

He would not have made man

But instead a world full of moles

Lately I have begun to think

Doomsday for mankind is not a myth

For it seems the car we are driving

Has been driven over the cliff

We should have started early

To stop it if we could

Applying the brakes now

Won't do us any good

Once it was thought that man

Could not deplete fish in the ocean

But pollutants and the last oil spill

Are doing it in one swift motion

It appears that the end is near

And I have much regret

For the extinction of all mankind

Seems to be our final kismet

Pick Up The Soap

Sagging pants wearers with your underwear showing

Do you even know if you are coming or going

I guess you must think that you look real cool

But you really look like a doggone fool

If you apply for a job wearing your sagging pants

People who hire won't give you a second glance

If you commit a crime, you'd better have a good plan

Because you can't even run from the policeman

If you try to run, you will trip up and fall

Then you will get a free ride to the jail near city hall

To appear before twelve people and a judge

Whose dislike for sagging pants will not budge

Then you will feel really stupid and dumb

When you are put in a place where sagging comes from

In prison, sagging may not mean what you intend

It means that who you really like are men

The pants are worn sagging for reasons best

Because it makes for quick and easy access

If this is not the image that you want to portray

Then maybe you should start dressing another way

Sagging pants are very uncouth and so unwise

Unless that is what you are trying to advertise

So if that is really your point and case

Then my message to you is a total waste

If you keep sagging, then maybe there is hope

That eventually you might get to pick up the soap

When Wry Goes Awry

When wry goes awry

Friendships don't have to die

When wry goes awry

I have yet to figure out why

Some people with a life set in stone

Don't have a life of their own

When wry goes awry

Don't fall prey to a lie

When wry goes awry

Don't poke others in the eye

Everyone has a different take

On what is real and what is fake

When wry goes awry

Keep your head to the sky

When wry goes awry

Keep friends and family nigh

Don't let others drown you

With bigotry and their tainted view

Try to be more understanding

And a little less demanding

If you receive hate, then return hate

You will end up with an empty plate

I will always have love and empathy

For those awry who are dear to me

Who Are You?????

When I first embraced you

I never took you for who

Could bring me so much joy

Just like a brand-new toy

You possessed this mystical touch

That made my blood rush

You were very difficult to meet

Twice as hard to greet

But once set in motion

You produced your magic potion

That lifted me up so high

Like the clouds in the sky

Then you became a roller-coaster ride

Like the ebb and flow of the tide

That plunged me down so low

With nowhere else to go

When you are right, it's great

When you are wrong, it's hate

You are sweet while it lasts

But bitter once it's past

You can be entertaining and amusing

Or complicated and confusing

It's hard to say when you began

No one knows where you will end

You are a myriad of different things

From uncouth paupers to royal kings

I can never figure the final outcome

Whether to be cheerful with you or glum

It is still worth the effort to try

Than to let a chance pass me by

To experience what to do or not do

And wonder..... WHO ARE YOU?????

The Great Lie

Don't ever ask me to run for the presidency

I would certainly never make it

When asked about my past affairs

I would have to lie and fake it

When asked did I smoke cigarettes and weed

I most assuredly would not tell

Instead I would tell a big ole lie

And say "No, I did not inhale"

When asked did I chase wild women

To do anything with really strange

I would be forced to lie

And say "No and I'll never change"

When asked about my former friends

And did they have a habit of drinking

Whoever the heck wrote these rules anyway

And whatever the heck were they thinking

The old Presidents did not follow these rules

Some had a Mrs. and a concubine

Some drank and had affairs openly

Like picking ripe grapes off the vine

Still they managed to run the country

In a somewhat accepted way

To control poverty and hunger

And keeping our enemies at bay

The modern Presidents have issues too

But they spin doctor them to bed

Even getting away with weird stuff

Like shooting their buddy in the head

Don't be quick to judge them

Because you don't share their same view

They are still just a person like you and me

With a big job ahead to do

Memories

As time marches on, everything will change

As years go by, this world will rearrange

Nothing will always stay as it is

Our sadness won't always bring tears

As the world spins on its axis

There will always be death and taxes

Even though now that you are gone

I still don't feel like I am alone

Memories of you still dance in my head

Each night as I lie in my bed

Then when I fall fast asleep

In my dreams you are mine to keep

If I said that I did not miss

The warmth of your tender kiss

It would be totally untrue

Because forever I will miss you

It is not really unusual or odd

That people love and then grow apart

People come and go for a reason

Just like the changing of the season

Even though we might not understand

Our parting seems to be of God's plan

He alone has the power to see

What the future holds for you and me

When I think of all of the good times we had

I can never be lonely or sad

To love you was a real pleasure

That left memories I will always treasure

Why Can't We All Get Together

Choosing a religion can become a joke

Kind of like having a pig in a poke

It is hard to distinguish between good and bad

When often the difference is merely a tad

If you praise the words of Jesus

Some will say they will not please us

If you swear by the almighty Allah

Some will say he won't get you by

If you worship a bountiful Buddha

You won't get what's due ya

If you are a devout Catholic

It still ain't the right pick

God doesn't care about the religions you choose

As long as you obey his basic rules

Like be good to your sisters and brothers

And respect your fathers and mothers

Whether you worship a tree or a rock

God is still with you around the clock

Just to believe plays a major part

In service to our omnipotent God

Who always hears our own personal pleas

And responds to our own special needs

I think that man created religions

To justify his own shortcomings and convictions

Each requiring different stipulations

All seeking the same expectations

We should rid ourselves of fears and doubt

And learn what other religions are about

Then work together for the same cause

And realize we all have the same boss

Then And Now

Thank God I made it to the sixties

With all of the things I went through

Although we did have lots of fun

We knew what to do and not do

When I was young and hardheaded

Doing the mischievous things I did

There are some things kept secret

From which my mother I hid

If she only knew some of the things

She would turn over in her grave

Like steal plums from the neighbors

Smoke pot and misbehave

If we got into a fight

Someone might pull out a knife

But it never escalated to the point

To kill and take a life

Kids today are much different

They have a lot to prove

They will plot a pipe bombing scheme

Then put the details on YouTube

Take AK47's and Glocks

To go shoot up their school

After they announce it on Facebook

To defy the golden rule

They play computer-generated games

With graphics so vivid and real

Which gives them the feel of power

While confirming their right to kill

The more graphic the games are

The more violent they become

We now have a race of kids

Left heartless, ruthless and numb

Our kids have a big problem

So let's give it our best

To steer them in the right direction

And let God handle the rest

3 Wheels 3 Women 3 Wishes

Whoever said that 2s company and 3s a crowd

Must have been born and raised on a farm

Everybody knows that whatever you do

The third time is always the charm

As you grow older, you will start to learn

To give in to the powers that be

Especially the basic law of nature

That makes good things happen in three

If your back and legs are giving you trouble

And you want to go shopping downtown

Buy a three-wheeled motorized scooter

To carry you and your packages around

It helps to have three women in your life

A caring nurse, a good cook and a tidy maid

Who will feed, cook and care for you

Provided from the benefits of Medicaid

A fairy godmother is not a bad idea

To grant you three wishes for last

To add a little zest to your future

And maybe even tweak your past

For wish one, I want to be young again

And take away all of my aches and pain

To be able to go walking and biking

Or go singing and dancing in the rain

I'd turn the nurse, cook and maid

Into three young ladies in hot pants

To provide a little exciting eye candy

And be partners in the rain dance

For us to get around town on

I'd wish for a Boom Mustang Trike

And tell my old motorized scooter

To take a well-deserved hike

We'd be drinking from gold-rimmed glasses

And eating from silver-plated dishes

But it's just an old man's foolish dream

3 wheels, 3 women and 3 wishes

A Doggone Shame

IT'S A DOGGONE SHAME

We as a diverse nation of people

Have traveled so far in time

To arrive in these present days

Where a hate shooting is not a crime

We drafted a new law stating

It's alright to defend yourself

If someone endangers your life

By risking your bodily health

This law can be interpreted

To apply to any situation

So even if you kill someone

You are granted emancipation

IT'S A DOGGONE SHAME

We live in a wicked world

Where someone could kick in your door

Wrap you and your family with duct tape

Face down on the stone cold floor

Asking you things you don't know

Leaving your life in a mess

Searching your house for valuables

That you don't even possess

Taking anything they can

Or what comes into their sight

To quench their thirst for violence

And ensure their greedy plight

IT'S A DOGGONE SHAME

The economic situation we face

Is a well-thought-out plan

By the current powers that be

To control our supply and demand

IT'S A DOGGONE SHAME

The Perplexing Paradox Of Love

How can you love someone

While despising who they are

Desire someone

Yet push them away

The paradox of love

Is perplexing

Like fire embracing ice

While still remaining ablaze

Two total opposites of nature

Existing symbiotically in a moment

With one's survival weighing totally upon

The exhaustion or depletion of the other

Precariously nestled between fire and ice

Lies a melting or freezing point

Reminiscent of great past loves

And present loves unrequited

Teetering and toddling

To and fro back and forth

Struggling to keep an even keel

To keep things afloat

Seemingly yet to hold sway

One way or another to stabilize

Is the total worth sum of love

Just a paradoxical roller-coaster ride

Perched upon the narrow precipice

Of hopes, dreams, doubt and abhorrence

Like fire embracing ice????

Love is blind is often said

But after loving and hating

Comes learning and acceptance of

The Perplexing Paradox

Of Love

Upside Down

Why do our minds change the time to DLS

Without letting the body know

When the mind awakes the next morning

The body is not ready to go

The body is not that stupid

It knows when it's time to wake up

When the mind wakes it up early

It makes the day a little rough

Ben Franklin thought about DLS

Way back in 1784

Apparently people were smarter then

Because it did not become status quo

Then a fellow named George Hudson

Proposed it again in 1895

That is when people got stupid

And day light saving came alive

Maybe then it was a good idea

To change the time around

But now in these modern times

It is looked upon with a frown

When you awake an hour early in spring

Then sleep an hour late in the fall

It only brings confusion to the mind

And the body doesn't like it at all

The only people who it does not affect

Are babies and retirees

Because to them, time is irrelevant

And they wake up when they please

They don't care what day it is

Nor worry about the time

To awake their bodies early

Is a serious punishable crime

We all need to wise up

And stop changing the time around

Before we end up like babies

With our sleeping patterns upside down

Mrs Fountain

I would love to find me a Deborah

Someone to love forever and ever

Someone who is comfortable in her own skin

Not to ever question where I've been

Who can hang out with me and the boys

Or play with the grandkids and their toys

Whose love is designed to elevate

Never to hinder, stifle or suffocate

Who always has a master plan

To aid and support her loving man

Though she is the woman of every man's dream

My intentions are not what they seem

I know she is true and the "real deal"

Because she is married to my friend Phil

The Love Blender

(BLUES SONG)

My baby makes love like a high-speed blender

She is truly just one of a kind

To make sure everything is in place

She starts with a low-speed GRIND

As things get to sparking

And our engines start to purr

She changes her body motion

To a medium-speed STIR

As the mixture gets moving

From a WHIP to a PUREE

She shifts her gears again

To a BLEND and a FRAPEE

Right when I can't stand any more

And start saying my my my

She ends it in high speed

Going straight to LIQUEFY

She really knows how to love me

And mix it up real funky

To drive me out of my mind

Making me scream like a howler monkey

When we are through making love

She switches to MARINADE

Which isn't a blender setting

But it keeps her bills paid

Helter Skelter

Every day you notice

    Some of your friends are gone

        Wakes you up at night

    Feeling all alone

Reality starts sinking in

    We all are slowly dying

        Reports from your doctor

Make you feel like crying

    Drugs, smoking and drinking

        For a quick relief

    Only result in

A much later grief

    Pills for your blood pressure

        And high cholesterol

    Ain't good for your liver

Or your kidneys at all

    To treat one symptom

Causes side effects in another

It's HELTER SKELTER

Where is my mother???

It is not funny

What can you do

Doctors in it for the money

Who you can't sue

Where do you go

Who do you trust

It's all a big game

But die you must

Pick your own poison

Of how to die

Because the inevitable end

Will soon be nigh

Until then keep on living

Slough away your fears

Celebrate the good times

It is what it is

Enjoy each day you're given

As though it is your last

Hope for the future

Keep memories of the past

All About Nothing

Some people who brag about what they can do

Are lost in this world without a clue

You say that you can do this and that

But you really don't know where it's at

You claim to have so much power

But you will never be the man of the hour

You say that you have lots of skill

But you don't even know what's real

You are just a product of your environment

Confused and addled with no good intent

You say you will show me what you can do

But don't show me, you need to show you

I have already made my cheese

There is no one who I am trying to please

But if you won't listen to what I have to say

Then you need to go on about your merry way

If you really do possess one of God's gift

Then you need to use it now and be swift

For time waits around for no man

So get up off of the ground and make a stand

If you want to stand tall and upright

Believe in yourself with all of your might

God put some people in your life just for

The sole purpose of being your mentor

But if you want to remain ignorant and blind

This world will definitely leave you behind

In your life, no grapes you will be busting

On the real tip, you are just all about nothing

My Three Loves

I would love to love as I've done before

To love somebody forever more

I would love to love as I have before

But lately my love is behind a swinging door

Guarded by feelings of deep regret

Left by the last attempt of love I met

So far the forces of nature that be

Have relegated me to a love of only three

Three women of such poise and beauty

Who made loving them my solemn duty

They were all fun and very first rate

Making it hard for others to duplicate

When you have loved and had the best

You find it hard to settle for less

But their loves have now come and gone

Leaving behind no hard feelings to bemoan

Though our relationships ended with tears

They taught me what love really is

If I never get another love like the three

I'll be satisfied with loving just me

Trash Talking Ways

There was once a fellow from North Carolina

Who moved to Georgia when he was just a minor

He was not smart enough to be an oceanographer

So he went to school to be a photographer

He landed a job at Lockheed after a photo session

Worked hard and rose to the top of his profession

They paid him well and flew him all over the land

To be the best at his profession was his plan

His signature look was a big, black, groomed mustache

And from under it came plenty of smack talking trash

Often with his trash talking I would try to compete

But his was honed to an art that no one could beat

Yep, you had to be on your toes when he came around

Or else against his trash talking, you would lose hands down

He retired and bought a high-dollar camera by Leica

And a new Trek 24 speed bike to be a biker

He travels around taking pictures near and far

Sometimes stopping for a drink at a neighborhood bar

Since now his big, black, groomed mustache has turned gray

He got tired of dying it black, so he shaved it away

The world is now his oyster at his beck and call

He has money, homes, toys, fast cars, he has it all

But his main love is still talking trash to drive you ape

To make you want to cover his mouth with duct tape

When we meet, we have fun rehashing the good old days

Of Lockheed, friends, family, foes and our trash talking ways.

I would not trade these meeting for any price

Because talking trash and laughter is the spice of life

God's Math

Winter as planned slowly creeps in

To devoid us of the sun's lights

And leaves with us in its wake

Cold rainy days and freezing nights

It strips the trees bare of leaves

And freezes the ponds and lakes

It makes the ground cold as ice

And increases my pains and aches

Though the scourge of winter seems harsh

Often beyond all practical reasons

It is necessary like some events in life

To complete all of the seasons

Our lives operate in a deviating cycle

Like fall, winter, spring and summer

Sometimes it is all aflutter like spring

Sometimes it is a cold winter bummer

I have learned when I encounter times

Stricken with the cold winter blues

God gives us a mathematical formula

To provide warmth and comfort to use

Add together your good and bad times

Then divide the total by two

You will come up with an average

Of your life events to review

Now take these and compare them

To some people who you know

It might give you a new perspective

To give what you have another go

So when you feel really weighed down

Snowed in by the winters of despair

Take time out to do his math

Remember that God allows you to tare

The "Itis" Boys

It is the ides of January 2019

I am still relevant on the scene

Today I am 67 years old

While having a problem doing what I'm told

I don't have to be in the bed by ten

To drink and smoke is not a sin

I can stay in my PJs all day

Just because "I GOT IT THAT WAY"

I can come and go as I please

"UNLESS" I have a flare-up in my arthritic knees

Then I have to do what they say

Just because "THEY GOT IT THAT WAY"

It's an excruciating pain unlike no other

That will make you scream for your mother

Nothing ruins your day like arthritis

Or his lil brothers tendinitis and bursitis

When the "ITIS" boys come to town

Your whole day is completely shut down

Then most of your time you will consume

Limping from the bed to the bathroom

Dr. C.

It is still January of the same year

I want to make this abundantly clear

If you want to keep your pain at bay

Please go and see Dr. C. today

He gave me a shot in my knee

And I did not even flinch or pee

When it comes down to managing pain

Dr. C. is "As Right As Rain"

Thank you, Thank you Dr. C.

I am now as happy as can be

You made the "ITIS" boys go away

Just because "YOU GOT IT THAT WAY"

Gardenias And Gladiolus

(Dedicated to Blanche Williams)

Fresh cut flowers remind me of when

I was growing up with my best friend

A friend who taught me right from wrong

How to be safe, positive and strong

A friend who taught me about life

Not to worry about its strife

Gardenias and Gladiolus were their favorite flowers

That would scent the house for hours and hours

They would put Gardenias in a big bowl

Then fill it with water to make them hold

Place the Gladiolus in a large vase

Filled with water to their taste

With my friend and these flowers in the house

I feared nothing I came across

I knew that everything was alright

So I slept soundly all through the night

My friend took care of everything I would need

From a broken heart to a nosebleed

A friend who was like no other

Who just happened to be my darling mother

With me being the only child

My life with her was exciting and wild

We went everywhere together

Rain, sunshine or stormy weather

I trusted her for eats and treats

Until she made me eat some nasty red beets

She told me they were good for me

Today I still totally disagree

Although she is gone, she will always be near

As long as Gardenias and Gladiolus are here

To remind me of her loving face

And bless me with God's holy grace

Ya Done Real Good

Obama Obama ya done real good

You ran this country like nobody else could

You cleaned up the mess left by the last administration

Restored this country back to greatness with no hesitation

To a place we are proud to live in and love

With the help and approval of our mighty God above

You set an example for all the people of the world to see

To have hope of what they can achieve and be

You did this in spite of being diametrically opposed

By the Republican Party, congressional constituents and foes

Who would cut off their nose to spite their face

Than see you occupy your rightful space

As the supreme ruler of the known free world

And an inspiration for our young boys and girls

I'm not saying that you are a perfect president

There's probably lots of decisions that you resent

But I think you did the best that you could do

Considering the situation that was left to you

And just because your skin is black

Was no reason for you to come under attack

From people who did not want to believe

That you did most of what you set out to achieve

It is sad to see after eight years you have to go

I wish we could change the law to give you eight more

In eight more you could make the world a better place

For our living planet and the entire human race

True Friendship Prologue

I have learned in my older age that friendship

is not measured only by how close you are to someone.

It is measured in the number of years you are close to someone.

I guess it's the reason, season or lifetime thing.

You can have a close friend who you see every day that might end abruptly

or a close friend who you might see often or every blue moon that lasts forever.

I have been fortunate enough to have the latter

who I cherish and trust with my innermost thoughts and feelings

after "PRUTTNEAR" (pretty near) 50 years of friendship.

A mere poem cannot express or represent my gratitude of this friendship but

HERE IT IS

You know who you are and don't need to be named to define yourself.

True Friendship

I have a friend I've known for most of my life

We get together and trade worthwhile advice

On worldly topics of things that matter

Right down to how to make cake batter

Sometime we shoot the bull for fun

After all the serious issues are done

But mostly we are true to the cause

With no stones unturned or lost

Although we disagree on lots of stuff

Our conversation has never gotten rough

To the point of causing an argument

Or bringing to the other bad intent

We speak with words we do not mince

That are from the heart and often intense

We always agree to disagree

Letting all things be as they be

We disagree on theories of religions

Because of our preconceived convictions

But we both agree that without God

There is no real just reward

We share lots of interests and taste

Agree that haste always makes waste

We were both born in a hospital named Grady

We each got married twice to the same lady

We played together in the high school band

Always ready to lend each other a hand

We are both highly competitive and like to win

We both play the game of life to the end

The only time that our friendship becomes unstable

Is on the chess board or the pool table

Only then he's not my friend at all

But merely just the next victim to fall

Dark Ages

As I sat alone in darkness

Due to Mother Nature's storm

Trying to entertain myself

By any fashion or form

No TV, No DVR, No Internet

Only me and my imagination

If this is the "Way It Used to Be"

This was a terrible situation

No TV, No DVR, No Internet

How did early man survive

Having no HBO or Showtime

To order or subscribe

I went into my office

With some thoughts to write

But it just ain't the same

While trying to hold a flashlight

Early man wrote on cave walls

By the light of a campfire

Using a burned stick for a pen

That I can really admire

Now we make paper from trees

For magazine and book pages

TVs, DVRs and Internet

To keep us from the Dark Ages

We have gas and electricity

For heating, cooking and light

Security cameras and cell phones

To me this is just right

But they ain't worth a hoot

When Mother Nature rages

Taking away gas and electricity

Putting us back in the Dark Ages

Now I See The God In Me

For so long I felt empty inside

because I had nothing to fill that void.

I thought that having people around would fill it.

For so long, everyone fell short of that goal

and the emptiness remained.

Now I finally know how to fill the void in me

Now I finally see the God in me.

No one can fill the void in you

but the God in you.

So be kind to you and "DO YOU."

If we are from God, then God is within us.

Free yourself from yourself to find yourself

as the God within you demands.

Don't overburden yourself with man's written rules

that you think God needs fulfilled.

God requires no written rules to follow.

God's requirements are intuitive and simple.

God requires no collection of monies in his name

to sate the wishful urges of certain individuals

who self-appoint themselves as God's representatives.

Stop being a slave to religions

for God requires no servitude and is not jealous.

Jealousy is a human emotion

that leads to self-destruction as a result of self-doubt.

Be confident in your decisions

for you can be your own worst judge and jury of yourself.

You know when you do wrong or right

and punish or reward yourself accordingly.

Realize and trust the God in you

to guide you through times of self-doubt.

Be the God in you as God intended you to be.

You will be pleasantly pleased with life

Once you start believing in

THE GOD IN YOU.

Just Thoughts

(SHEPHERDS AND SHEEP)

Be not dismayed when doors close

It is often needed to open another

Never hold on to somebody

Just to have someone

In the end, you are left

With no one

Count every day above the ground life

Every day below the ground another life

Never let anyone control your anger

Once you get shook, you get took

Be the cream not the crud

Once stirred, rise to the top

In this world of shepherds and sheep

Make "BLEATING" sure

You know which one you are

Then graze accordingly

Sometimes you are a sheep

Sometimes you are a shepherd

While you are a sheep

Be obedient and follow

While you are a shepherd

Take charge and lead the flock

Don't Tell Don't Ask

People are always complaining

About the hard facts of life

Of their health and wealth

Their moments of strife

When people ask you

How do you feel

They don't want to hear

About your woes and ills

They want to hear something

Nice and encouraging

Not woefully sad

And utterly discouraging

A life without obstacles

Like a rose without thorns

Is a mad raging bull

You will never grab its horns

Life is meant to live

Not to complain

Suck up the small stuff

And your sanity will remain

Every one of us has

Our own distinct ways

Mountain goats climb

Low-land sheep graze

A mountain without cracks

Is very hard to scale

So if you don't like heights

Stay in the dell

Bridging The Gap

There's not much difference between rap and poetry

They both tell about life's stories

But rap seems to get all of the "bad raps"

While poetry seems to get all of the glories

Rap is "mostly" written by one culture

Poetry is "mostly" written by others

When it comes right to it

They are just brothers from different mothers

I would like to introduce a style

That has recently occurred to me

That's a cross between the two

That I affectionately call rappetry

Rappetry don't need no editing

To put in the periods and commas

You can write any way you want

Even bout yo babies' mommas

Rappetry is not new on the scene

It just never had a real name

I intend to change all of this

By bringing it to its due fame

Because I make things rhyme

I have been criticized by folks

Who said my writings are childish

Lousy and full of jokes

If this rappetry style catches on

To achieve its overdue rank

I will keep on writing like this

Joking all the way to the bank

Poets write lines without prose

Rappers write lines with rhymes

But this style I call rappetry

Is a sign of the new times

HOLLA!!

Learning vs Earning

Let me tell you about lessons learned

Which are different from lessons earned

Lessons learned are from book readings

Lessons earned come from life's teachings

The big difference between the two

Is what life's lessons deliver to you

Opposed to what you read and receive

Based on which book readings you believe

Book readings are for you to learn

Life's lessons are for you to earn

The lessons your parents instilled in you

Will eventually come into view

From the things you thought were dumb

Not realizing where they were coming from

They helped you form your life

By giving you sound advice

From the mistakes they made

And the high prices they paid

To earn what they found to be true

Because of their love for you

If you listened, you would have learned

About the lessons that they earned

Putting you on a path of earning

From all of your past learning

Then when you are grown

Having children of your own

You can teach them to learn

What life taught you to earn

Our Creations

Our youth are facing a terrible battle

Going up the creek without a paddle

They are so busy seeking their thrills

With liquor, powder and popping pills

To realize what's right or wrong

Or see what's coming at them head-on

They are busy trying to steal and rob

Instead of seeking a good paying job

Our youth are too trusting to see

Their parents were an unknown enemy

Who filled them full of all kinds of meds

In order to maintain their level heads

With drugs like Ritalin and Prozac

Then expected them to socially interact

When shipped off to faraway schools

Mass producing young educated fools

As youth, they saw us smoking and drinking

What in the hell were we thinking

If you want to hear the real truth

We made them drug addicts as youth

When the real ounce of prevention

Was merely giving them our attention

We were so busy trying to earn a living

That we neglected the love we were giving

Although we really meant well

We have made their lives a living hell

We can change this by giving them love and hugs

Instead of Ritalin, Prozac and prescription drugs

Watch Out For Cars Dummy

Have you ever done something that wasn't very smart

Something you knew was dumb from the start

But you dove right in and did it anyway

Hoping that somehow your dumb plans would pay

Your dumb luck with high dividends

Allowing you to impress all your friends

But as usual when your dumb plans failed

All your buddies tucked tails and bailed

Leaving you alone, high and dry

Trying to figure out how, when and why

Your dumb plans really backfired

Making you dumbfounded and mired

In debt and problems waist-deep

For only you to solve and reap

Tell yourself to finally admit it

You knew it was dumb when you did it

You knew it was a dumb shot in the dark

Not a safe, sure walk in the park

Like a dumb dog running after a car

You knew the time wasn't very far

When sooner or later like dumb old Rover

You might slip, fall and get run over

When you heal a little and the dumb is gone

Lick your wounds, tuck your tail and move on

Sometimes it's worth it, sometimes it ain't

Accept the outcome without complaint

Then maybe these dumb things you won't repeat

When the next car comes down the street

Friend, Project Or Foe

I have learned in my adult life that people categorize and see others as one of three types. Either you are a friend, a project or a foe. Your knowledge and experience in life makes you label people accordingly.

A friend is someone you accept as they are and the relationship remains as long as there is a mutual understanding respectfully for the differences in thinking and customs. This relationship is healthy for both parties, offering a chance for open-minded individuals to learn and grow from each other.

A project is someone you accept as a friend with a hidden agenda to change or "save" them from themselves and open their eyes to your "correct" ways of thinking. If you don't see it their way, the relationship abruptly ends.

A foe is someone you make after the project fails and you label them the scourge of the earth for not seeing things your way. Going from friend to foe produces a negative emotion of hate and envy. I wish everyone could just stay friends and let God make all of the judgment calls.

FRIENDS INSPIRE YOU TO ACHIEVE

THE GOALS THAT YOU BELIEVE

NOT HATE YOU FOR NOT HEEDING

WHAT THEY THOUGHT YOU WERE NEEDING

Forward To The Good Old Days

If I had to go back to the good old days

I would be where I am right now

When I want milk for my cereal

I don't wanna have to milk no cow

When they say things were better back then

They must not have given the thought

That everything that was needed and used

Was either handmade or bartered, not bought

Back then if you wanted a new suit to wear

To your wedding a couple of months away

You needed to shop for the material

Then start sewing on it that day

Today when you need a suit to wear

You go to the mall or K&G

The selection of clothes that they have

Can make you dapper as can be

Back then if you had boars and cows

And I had sows and a bull

After all of the bartering went down

Both of our smokehouses were full

Now when I want to fill up my freezer

I go to the Krogers or the Walmarts

For a couple of hundred dollars

I can fill up one or two carts

I don't think times will get any better

Until they make flying space cars

Then I will be able to go riding

On Jupiter, Saturn or Mars

Until then the good old days are right here

And what you are doing right now

If you disagree and want milk

Then go buy yourself a cow

O Where O Where!!!!

O where O where did January go

O where O where is all of the snow

Why did all of the cold weather stop

Why won't the temperature drop

It is hot enough to cook eggs on the street

With a side order of bacon for meat

Is this all because of an aerosol can

Or because of our huge oil demand

If these are the causes of global warming

It's not only ourselves who we are harming

Santa Claus might not have a place to live

Because the Arctic icecaps are about to give

Even the animals don't have a place to stay

Because we clear cut all of the trees away

What in the world were we thinking

To contaminate the water we are drinking

Who did we think we would deceive

By polluting the very air we breathe

It's getting to where you can't even sneeze

Without spreading some kind of disease

God made the earth to be man's asylum

Now he is about to vote us off the island

If this was one of our God's tests

We failed and made a big ole mess

I am not mad and I do understand

For us to destroy the earth was not his plan

I think it's time we all go live in a bubble

Because we are all in a heap of trouble

Sandcastles

Life is like the boundless ocean

On a calm day smooth as silk

With a tendency to go bad

Like nonrefrigerated milk

The tides of hope often crash

Upon the rocky shores with life

Engulfing sandcastles in its wake

Leaving behind misery and strife

Our dreams are the sandcastles

Sometimes awash in life's floods

Making us feel hopeless

At a loss for meaningful words

Don't despair and assign blame

For we did nothing wrong

It is all part of God's plan

To make us faithful and strong

As sure as the tides roll in

They must eventually roll out

Making our dreams stronger

To trust him without a doubt

Often our sandcastle dreams

Need to be washed away

For us to build anew

In hopes for a brighter day

Then we built new dreams

On a solid firm ground

Far away from the shore

Keeping us safe and sound

Remember as the tides ebb low

They eventually will flow high

If you build on high ground

Your sandcastles will stay dry

For Money Do We Part

Today's marriages are not just a love act

But a legally binding prenuptial contract

Replete with rules about what you should or should not do

Less concerned about who you see or woo

They more protect money and possessions we have

So that when one leaves, they don't up and grab

Possessions they didn't have when they came

To seek out instant money, fortune and fame

Back in the day, we married for supposedly true love

Believed sanctioned from God almighty above

How did we get from there to here

When did the money and possessions game appear

How do you know when it's time to move on

When can you be sure that true love is gone

Is the price of true love getting much too high

For a lifetime of commitment to honor and buy

Can you get it with a written guarantee

That true love will always stay as it be

To remain forever comforting and pure

Like in a fairy tale safe and sure

Fairy tales are safe for love to keep

Until you awaken from your somberly sleep

True love never fades is often said

That's really a cliché just being read

In a feeble attempt to fool one's mind

That true love is sweet and money blind

Marriages of modern true love depend on many things

Mostly possessions and money to the table one brings

Money draw money is the new real deal

You can't dine a princess with a Happy Meal

The Journey

From the beginning of God's creation

We have been driven by our imagination

Traveling through the streets of our minds

Paved by chance while ignoring stop signs

Down blind alleys of vivid dreamscape

Running wide open while not wide awake

To a destiny not chartered or shown

To arrive on time to a date unknown

Starting with a just a single breath

Signifying life with good health

Negativity adds to our journey's demise

Negated by lifestyle, diet and exercise

This journey is not always smooth sailing

Often navigated while sick and ailing

Through sunny days and hurricane winds

Until our street or road finally ends

Struggling to breathe one last desperate gasp

Succumbing to death's unrelenting grasp

At the front door of the grim reaper's domain

With feelings of utter disdain

How many journeys no man will know

It is not man's choice to stay or go

As sure as man lives, he shall perish

The life he lives, he should learn to cherish

Never have a worry, fret or fear

Because death is not the final frontier

Matter can be neither created nor destroyed

Which connects the death to life void

So no matter how life will end

It goes back to where it began

The Garden Tool

Why is it so hard to say no to

A certain woman who always abuses you

Why is there always just one girl

Who seems to corrupt your world

That makes you jump through a hoop

While doing a backward loop the loop

When you think the relationship is dead

She takes you back out of the shed

Drags you all through the recent dirt

Bringing back all of the past hurt

Hurt that you hate to relive and feel

But you can't deny yourself the thrill

Of being with her once again

Thinking maybe this time you'll win

Her heart for you forever and ever

To her it is always never and never

Then she puts you back in the shed to when

She decides to want to use you again

Just like an ordinary garden tool

I guess I'm just a masochist fool

Sometimes I get mad and run away

Only to come back the following day

I just can't seem to understand

Whether I am a mouse or a man

Maybe one day I will get hip

And try to break her fatal grip

Until then I will keep on getting used

Digging deep, put up dirty and abused

Hear Me Out!!!!!

Of all of the people in this world

I love to hear myself the most

I don't have a famous talk show

Of which I am the host

I don't give opinionated views

For all of the world to hear

That's on the air live broadcasted

All over far and near

But because I am not famous

And do not have a talk show

My opinions fall on deaf ears

And few will ever know

Still I love to listen to myself

And take heed to my own choice

Even the poor and homeless

Take pride to hear their own voice

To exist without worldly possessions

Costing money and promoting stress

Working a daily nine-to-five job

Just to give Uncle Sam the rest

They hear themselves just as much

As the people in Beverly Hills

Who get their thrills and kicks

From Botox and prescription pills

I don't think that they are any happier

Than the homeless living in a tent

The main difference I see is

The rich pays a bigger rent

To hear yourself is not insane

And certainly not a sin

To take heed a true voice

That comes from deep within

Lottery Player's Blues

Up at dawn

Home at dusk

Work, work, work

You must

On a penny-ante job

At best

Then you come home late

To eat and rest

Slave all week long

Then what you make

You don't ever see

After the government's take

Leaving just enough money

To get back to your job

Clothe and feed your family

Keep warm and not starve

Nothing extra

To put away

For the future

Or a rainy day

It's a vicious cycle

That I must do

Because all of my big plans

To hit the lottery keep falling through

Even though I play

Faithfully every day

My numbers get close

But they never fall my way

That's the way it is

It's not new news

Just an average day

With the lottery player's blues

A Final Lament

When I die don't mourn for me

Because I brought death on myself

I choose to live haphazardly

Knowing it would end with bad health

I was the one drinking and drugging

Having wild unprotected sex

Never giving it a second thought

Considering what could come next

I was the one speeding in my car

While sitting on the seat belt

Knowing if I had a fatal crash

For family it would be heartfelt

Even though this is an exaggerated truth

Our death would actually be stealing

Our friends' and families' dreams

For us who they were feeling

Our lives are intrinsically intertwined

Genetically from our fathers and mothers

To include, affect and influence change

On our family, friends and others

Our death might leave a void

In some lives that we were filling

Even as just a conversation piece

To keep their lives more thrilling

They might have a special memory

That they would want to share

To tell to our friends and family

To show how much they care

Tales of leading a wonderful life

The contributions we were giving

About being faithful to our spouse

The Christian life we were living

Regardless of the tales being spun

Circulating the rumor mill

We live and die at our own expense

Now that's the real deal

Miracles

Today I witnessed some miracles

As stunning as could be

I witnessed an orange sun set

Into the deep blue sea

I witnessed twinkling stars

Come out one after another

Until they filled the sky

Til I could see no further

I witnessed a yellow crescent moon

Traipse across the starlit sky

As a sparkling shooting star

Went quickly streaming by

The next morning I awoke

To a wonderful surprise

I witnessed song birds singing

And a big yellow sun rise

These are some basic miracles

That our God created

With such elegant beauty

Which are definitely underrated

These might not be miracles to you

But these are miracles to me

Every day that I arise

There is a miracle to see

If you open your eyes

You'll see miracles every day

If you open your heart

They will come your way

Then every day you awake

If that day is promised to you

Is for you to bear witness

To a miracle made anew

Trying To Change

I am new at writing poetry

Noticing that all poems don't rhyme

I am sure that I can adopt this style

If I am given a little more time

I am recently trying to express myself

With words that are somewhat dense

To create a poem without rhyme

Which doesn't make any sense

I have read a few poems

Without rhyme which are deep

Others I will never understand

With nothing tangible to reap

Poetry needs to stir one's soul

Fulfill something you're needing

Take you on an adventure

While providing something worth reading

Poetry is a poet's self-expression

Reaching into their inner soul

Extending the depths of their being

For their readers to behold

Perhaps one day I will catch on

Then write like most of the masses

To be in the upper echelon

And reach into the higher classes

Then maybe I am just a man

Doomed to be who I am

Destined to write with rhyme

Who doesn't give a damn

One day I will evolve

To write poetry without rhyme

Until then just bear with a brother

And give me a little more time

Why I Write

Writing puts my mind's deepest thoughts

Of my innermost being from my past and present

In front of my innocent eyes

To behold and judge as fact or fiction

Be aware of what you dredge up from the past

Some things will define your future

Some things will continue to destroy your present

I am who I am with no regrets

Everyone doesn't agree with what I write about

But I am not asking for their approval for me

To express myself in my writings

All I ask for is a small window into their minds

To question and answer whether there is some truth

And enjoyment to be gleaned without being biased or ignorant

If you are biased, quit reading; if you are ignorant, fact-check me

My belief is, if you're not living on the edge

Then you're taking up too much space

In a universe replete with nothing but space

If I don't write to the edge of my creative ability

How would I know my space limitations' extremities

The only way is to go there and scale back

To a happy acceptable medium

It takes lots of chutzpah to express yourself in writing

Knowing that you're at the mercy of others

Judging you as either

A narcissistic psychopath or a choir boy

But yet ink still continues to flow

From my pen to my paper daily

I WRITE

As a testament of my commitment

To express my sincere gratitude

For my God-given gift in writing

COGITO ERGO SUM

(I think therefore I am)

"Bestest Of Friends"

In 1975, I crossed paths

With a very pretty young girl

Who blossomed into a beautiful sexy woman

Who altered and redefined my world

At first there was no attraction between us

Definitely not love at first sight

But fate's irony joined us together

To produce a magic union just right

Then we became madly in love

Just like in a storybook fairy tale

She was my queen and I was her king

And all throughout, the land was well

We married and had two fine children

Who made the magic tale complete

Who blessed us with four grandkids

For a much added treat

Time moved on and the magic waned

As life presented itself to unfold

We divorced and went our separate ways

But we never forgot our common goal

To keep our families' legacy intact

For our grandkids, daughter and son

So on special occasions and birthdays

We still come together as one

To ensure our family structure is sound

To have fun as a family

Despite our different views

We still enjoy each other's company

I will always support her and our kids

From now until this world ends

Even after being married and divorced twice

We are still the "Bestest of Friends"

Doubting And Doing

Everyone doesn't have the same drive

When it comes to gaining success

Some aim for the moon and stars

Others could not care less

Successful people are highly confident

They have no room for doubt

When one avenue seems closed

They just take another route

Doubt is the biggest enemy

That keeps success at bay

Once doubt is here and present

Your dreams suddenly melt away

Some people have big dreams

Some people don't

Some people will succeed

Some people just won't

It is totally up to you

To choose your own lot in life

But if you are somewhat skeptical

Here's a little advice

STOP DOUBTING

AND START DOING

TO ACHIEVE THE DREAMS

YOU ARE PURSUING

Your dreams will not mature

Unless you plant a positive seed

Then nourish it with assured confidence

To blossom into a successful deed

Let's Come Together

Why does everyone in the world pretend

To belong to different races when

Right now in this time in space

There is only one human race

Humans all come from only one descent

Being from the African continent

Even if your ancestors come from Antarctica

Their roots still started in Africa

We are all inherently the same

So let's pull together and take aim

For everybody to unite as one

Hoping for better days on this planet to come

What would it take to get people to see

Even if we just simply agree to disagree

We can still all come together

To make this world a whole lot better

Start fretting with the shape the planet is in

Instead of the color and hue of another's skin

Put bigotry, hatred and racism aside

To deal with the world's problems in stride

It seems the only way to love each other

Is to breed until we are all the same color

Everyone would be a nice caramel shade

Then nobody would know who to invade

I think it would be more intelligent

Just to deem color to be irrelevant

If we start now, it might not be too late

To avoid our impending doom of fate

My Wish

If I could wish my life to do over

I would not change a thing

I would not wish for fancy cars

Or the Blue Hope Diamond Ring

I accept things the way they are

With no regrets for the past

I awake every day to live

By how the dice are cast

If they roll not in my favor

I do not cause alarm

I will accept an unfavorable outcome

With grace, poise and calm

If I could wish my life to do over

I would not wish for wealth

I would only wish for God's blessing

To keep me in good health

The Give And Take Of It All

It's a known fact that everybody doesn't believe

It is better to give than receive

People are often divided into two makes

One always gives, while the other always takes

A taker can never be a giver

They are selfish with nothing to deliver

Givers can never be takers

They are sincere and often peacemakers

There exists a distinct line of demarcation

When it comes to each one's conversation

When takers talk, they talk a lot

It's like trying to talk to a robot

They never hear a word you say

They will never ask "How was your day"

They will offer you goo-gobs of advice

On how to improve your life

Their conversation is brassy and bold

It turns you off and makes you cold

Now a giver should be a national treasure

Talking to them is a rewarding pleasure

Their conversation is true and warm

They are helpful and won't cause harm

A giver can talk you from the valley of depression

To the top of the mountain of resurrection

Givers give you something to reap

Like words of wisdom to keep

So when the takers are around to make you yawn

Keep a giver around for wisdom and fun

The Cup

Most of us are conditioned by our society

To accept certain norms as a top priority

Like taking the yearly flu shot vaccine

That has a hidden agenda behind the scene

It never seems to prevent the flu

So what the hell does it really do

Even accepting those "free" government cell phones

Thinking that you really control its offs and ons

Without doing due diligence due

From an investigative point of view

Believe me it's always listening to you

While recording everything that you do

No need to implant your body with a chip

You just simply carry it on your hip

We take different medications for some pains

Only to end up with side effects and other "thangs"

That end up being way "MO" bad

And far "MO" worse than what you had

We are all in the Jim Jones Parade

Being conditioned to drink the Cup's Kool-Aid

Like calves marching to their slaughter

In perfect line and order

Without having a reason why

Marching only to believe and die

When will our society wake up

And stop drinking from The Cup

When will we learn to think on our own

And stop being a slave to someone else's throne

Neighbor 911

In every neighborhood, there exists the kind of neighbor

Who likes to get into everybody's Kool-Aid flavor

When they think that you are having too much fun

They will pick up the phone and report you to 911

They constantly seem to stay in a grouchy mood

Always trying to get someone locked up or sued

You really have to be aware and stay on guard

About something simple as your kids' ball in their yard

If your dog crosses over their property line

You and your dog might get slapped with a healthy fine

If your dog barks too loud when you're not around

He just might get sent to the local dog pound

If you play your music a little too loud

They will call the police without a doubt

Because they call the police about every little thing

The police have created for them their own special ring

They are used to Neighbor 911 calling and fussing

They know that their complaints are all about nothing

Their bothersome ways seem to be without cease

Surely there must be some way to find peace

I think the only way to keep one's sanity and sense

Is to build between them and us an eight-foot fence

One made of wood that is big and strong

Then there is no way they can accuse us of wrong

Maybe this will keep Neighbor 911 at bay

Then everyone can have a peaceful day

But if they still insist on being neighbor-haters

The next plan should be a moat filled with alligators

On A Zoom

As I zoom through spaces and times

Painting in and out of the lines

Blurred with visions I think I see

Of this opaque reality that just might be

I try to make sense of this illusion

Of mass mind-boggling confusion

By tapping the serenity of my mind

Not focused on a mere dollar sign

On paper with a dead president

Designed only to eat and pay rent

I arise every day to learn and live

What life's lesson has that day to give

Feeding nourishment to my brain

To keep my sanity from being insane

Continuing to resolve this life's future maze

From past thick clouds of smoke and purple haze

Just to die to achieve the ultimate goal

That results in "Eternal Life" I'm told

An apropos reward for where I've been

Zooming through anarchy, turmoil and sin

Maybe I'm just a Doubting Thomas

But I don't live life on a promise

I live life to enjoy each day

Not to squirrel and stash away

Waiting for death to bring a better life

That's picture-perfect and free of strife

Life is meant to live on a ZOOM

Anything else is just lying in a TOMB

The Family Tree

It is hard to be a real man

A wise old man once said

You may not even get recognized

Until you are cold and dead

The stairs that lead to manhood

Are hard, long and winding

That requires starting a family tree

To make your family spiritually binding

At the time when I first heard this

I was young and lost as can be

With no idea of how to be a father

Much alone starting a family tree

I was like a honey bee in a garden

Going from flower to flower

Never thinking about the consequences

Just living from hour to hour

Now all praise to the powers that be

I am the proud father of three

To be a real man, you need a job

To support you and your family

That makes a strong rooted trunk

Needed to grow your family tree

With your children as sturdy branches

To your trunk firmly attached

Provides a deep-seated family base

That can't be uprooted or detached

Then your family tree starts to bloom

With grandchildren as budding leaves

Laughing and playing in the sun

Growing stronger in the gentle breeze

Soon your tree will grow strong

Tall enough to reach the sky

To provide lots of family to love

For the future years to come by and by

At Sea

My woman, my lover, my foe

Or someone who I used to know

My man, my friend, my enemy

Just which will you eventually be

We waver like moths to a candle flame

Avoiding the fire to stay in the game

We try to play the game well

To make it hard for others to tell

We are living in a state of delusion

Bordering on total mass confusion

It will be just fine she would always say

As if our woes will miraculously go away

Taking with them the bad thoughts we hide

To mask our selfish human pride

While we play the happy couple card

Acting in this most unhappy facade

All of these roles confuse us

To the point of where we don't trust

Not knowing or being certain

What's behind the next curtain

Illuminating the stage for us so bright

As a starless unlit new moon night

Keeping us stumbling around in the dark

Looking for a peaceful place to park

Our true emotions and feelings

For necessary mental healings

Just as lost as lost can be

In gale storm winds out at sea

The Book Of KD

My life has been lived like an open book

With pages turned over by time

Even though some are tattered and torn

They are more valuable than a gold mine

In my youth, the pages turned slowly

For there was so much to learn

I lived my life on a whim haphazardly

As if I had pages to burn

Often I sit and reminisce

About events that turned each page

That filled in the empty lines

To arrive at this special age

Some pages written of past affairs

Inked in by woes and pain

Sprinkled with saddened tears

Like a slow drizzling rain

Tears of joy and happiness

Celebrated with glee and laughter

Producing very precious moments

To cherish forever after

As you age, your pages turn quickly

Like being blown by the wind

You notice your pages are filling

And your book is coming to an end

I am proud of every page

That unravels any mystery

Added to my book of life

Etching the annals of history

It is all there in black and white

For the whole world to see

Everyone has their book being written

Mine is The Book of KD

The Dust

Why are people so quick at a funeral to air

What the deceased were doing or saying

When in the end, the deceased are the only ones

For their consequences who are paying

For the broadcast deeds in life they did

Whether they were right or wrong

When the dust finally settles

It is their final swan song

With you being one of many

To perform on the next stage

With everyone else left remaining

Trying to rewrite their blank page

With no idea of how to think

Or even how to begin to say

How to express their last goodbyes

On their final given day

Eventually the dust

Will encompass all

No matter how big

Or how you have grown tall

The only redeemable aspect is

After the dust is complete

It provides another whole world

That is different and unique

For mankind to take notice

To be knowledgeable and not abuse

For those who bite the dust

To share their points of view

Spawned from our life's past experience

And the ashes of its inextinguishable fervor

For the betterment of our striving species

To perpetuate life forever and ever

Open Up

Open your mind to the obvious

Bare your soul to the truth

Some instead of opening their eyes

Would rather you pull their tooth

In these days of Internet information

The truth is there to share

For anyone who wants to learn

To make a difference if they care

Open your mind to the obvious

Step outside your comfort zone

Maybe you will learn some things

You thought right to be totally wrong

History has been edited and rewritten

By those now in power to be

What they want to have happened

And what they want the world now to see

The powers that be now

Have been waging a vicious war to win

Against truth, justice and equality

From their beginning to their unexpected end

Their first stage of waging their war

To win against their unsuspecting enemy

Was to create a cabal of allies

To believe their propaganda and agree

That the cause others are willing to die for

Is against the world's moral majority

And if they are allowed to exist

The results would be a worldwide catastrophe

They depend on their allies' ignorance

And their ability to not comprehend

For their victorious saving grace

And their enemies' final unsavory end

So study your own history in detail

To deny them their morbid pleasure

Of discrediting your own true history

Of being an aboriginal national treasure

KD's Knew Rules

#38574. Youngsters wearing their pants below their butts and privates in public shall be chased at random by a rabid, foaming-at-the-mouth pit bull dog until they learn where the running height of their pants is.

#38575. The next time you are awakened on your day off at 7:00 a.m. by the sound of someone ringing your doorbell trying to sell you something or sway your religious views, you should politely get their name and address so that on their next day off you can visit them at the same time to return the favor in kind.

#38576. Don't get upset because you heard about something derogatory someone said about you because all people spread gossip and you probably have said something derogatory about them as well in the past.

#38577. Show me a person who says they don't lie and I'll show you a big liar. Human instinct is to lie or fabricate details to their likings, whether it's a little white lie or a big ole black lie.

#38578. If you stir it up and it don't stink, it could be sugar. If you stir it up and it does stink, it's definitely not sugar!

#38579. The best way to keep a secret is to keep it in the circle of trust that only includes me, myself and I.

#38580. The difference between habits that are cute and adorable or degrading and obnoxious in a relationship depends on how long you have known each other.

#38581. Learn to keep your private thoughts to yourself. Some people use them as leverage to tell others to gain their trust to make them appear to be more important at your expense.

#38582. NEVER NEVER EVER post anything on Facebook at night after drinking four shots of hooch. The next morning you read it, you are left wondering...WHO WAS THAT MASKED MAN!!!

#38583. Some people who others think act funny are not that at all. They just have a very highly sensitive bullshit meter that is set between LOW and NO tolerance!

#38584. In this land of milk and honey, be the cream not the crud. When stirred, rise to the top because you only get took when you get shook!

#38585. Life and the game of Monopoly are alike because no matter how much money or how many car and houses you have managed to buy, at the end of each, they all go back in the box.

#38586. If you call someone and talk constantly for 15 minutes and all that your party says is "um hum" and "uh huh," then please give it a rest. Chances are they stopped listening to you after about 5 minutes of "um hums" and "uh huhs" and they don't know what the heck you are talking about anyway!

#38587. Getting some people to accept the truth is like using a fish hook to catch a fish....You just can't shove it down their throats, they have to want to swallow it!

#38588. One of the biggest joys you can bestow upon your parents is to succeed them in their given profession that they deemed an honorable living worth pursuing for the benefit of the family's survival, unless you have a better plan to improve on their time-honored choices to advance the standards for everyone in the family's future to come.

#38589. The difference between being smart enough to know and old enough to know is...Smart enough means that you are able to form a viable conclusion based on information and facts you received earlier to be true....Old enough means that the conclusion you were smart enough to conclude may be flawed and not worth a hill of beans.

#38590. The larger the pond you swim in, the more likely you are to come across fish like yourself.

#38591. Sometimes the best way to find out how much something weighs is to lay it down and let it rest.

Serenity Plea For Purpose

As I rise each morning, I give thanks

To the higher power that be

Knowing that my daily needs will be met

In kind accordingly

Though at times when shrouded in darkness

I am riddled with fear and doubt

Left aimlessly wondering

What my life's purpose is about

But somehow miraculously

My veil of darkness is lifted

Exposing me to the truth and light

Showing the purpose for which I am gifted

I don't know if everyone has

But I think that I definitely do

Possess a meaningful purpose to fulfill in life

With the help of my God's view

To navigate me through blind alleys

Up jagged hills of despair

As long as I have faith

My life's purpose will always be there

Until my intended mission is complete

And I pass the final test

Satisfying God's purpose in full

Allowing me to go to my final rest

The Creator's Love

O mighty stars that shine all night

Just to replicate our sense of day light

You were created to shine bright for all eternity

To allow our wondering eyes to see

The infinite beauty the Creator did provide

That is difficult to disguise, ignore or hide

He dwells in our very innermost being

Right down to our hearing and seeing

He makes the sun rise every morning in tune

With the setting of the stars and the moon

He makes the sea's tides ebb and flow

While sprinkling the mountain caps with snow

One would have to be vague and remiss

To not notice these wonders do exist

At the will of the Creator's master plan

That involves the love between a woman and a man

The love between our sisters and brothers

And our loving fathers and mothers

He created us to love unconditionally

Until those snowcapped mountains melt into the sea

Until all the rivers and streams run dry

And the moon and stars fall from the sky

His intentions were for us to love each other

Instead of causing strife and fighting one another

Somehow his plan seems to have gone awry

Considering all of the people we cause to die

If we don't learn to love each other some day

All of these wonders will eventually go away

When everyone realizes what the Creator's love has to give

This world will be a much nicer place in which to live

The Lies About Truth

How and why did the truth get busted

When did the truth get to be not trusted

It is now known as living proof

That the history we know ain't even the truth

Most of our history is riddled with lies

With lots of our world's leaders living in disguise

Hiding under their veil of secrecy

Pretending to be for the betterment of you and me

The public and the world are constantly under attack

Being repeatedly stabbed in the back

By people like these with forked silver tongues

Speaking from money-hungry filth-infested lungs

They belch out their greedy premeditated lies of deceit

Expecting everyone to sit down and feast

Feeding them lies and tales of the good ole days

Keeping their minds bogged down in a perpetual haze

Make no mistake, in the end it's all about the dollar

That's the only God that some of our leaders follow

Many of the world's crises and wars have been waged on lies

With us as the victors claiming the loser's wealth and prize

While killing their innocent women and children

Based on a self-righteous Hitler-inspired vision

As usual the winner and taker is all about us

Making us a nation that nobody in the world really trusts

When will all of the lies and killings come to an end

When will the real truth and trust to the world begin

Are there no scruples of our humanity left

To choose real truth over our country's ill-conceived wealth

The Human Struggle

The human struggle to survive is true and real

We live in a world of die or kill

The big dog always gets the big bone

The weak will never be king on the throne

When baby birds can't fly and fall to the ground

The cats and other predators quickly come around

To see what's on the bottom of the food chain

For the benefit of their species to sustain

It's just the natural order of the way things should go

To keep their species' quality of life in flow

Which allows only the strongest to remain alive

So that their species will prosper and survive

Mankind is the only species that goes against this creed

We will kill the strong to let the weak succeed

Not allowing some people needed to make a concession

For the benefit of the whole species' progression

We make these "who lives or dies" decisions

Based on things like skin colors and religions

We create a food chain from our discarded humanity

For those in power to feed on for their vanity

We destroy knowledge left by advanced past civilizations

That is essential for the development of new needed factions

We assassinate leaders who could benefit our future

Like Kennedy, Lincoln and the great Martin Luther

All in an attempt to distort and redirect our moral view

To give rise to only a select chosen few

Who have no interest in saving humanity as a whole

But who they can buy and sell with their huge payroll

When will our human species learn to decipher and choose

That without our species' humanities united, we all will lose

By judging each other by things like religion and skin color

That eventually leads to total annihilation of each other

Realization

Realization has prompted the wisdom in me

To unveil my closed eyes to see

When you are alone, you don't have to be lonely

You will always have you and you only

To bring your world into your own view

To do the things that you must eventually do

For the benefit of you and your health

To enjoy your hard-earned success and wealth

Money does not make the world go around

But the lack thereof makes some people frown

Often loving another will only take you so far

Like owning and driving a brand-new car

Sometimes when the maintenance and mileage builds

So does the decline of the frills and thrills

Which may leave you with you and only you

To make your wishes and dreams come true

Then if true happiness is what you really seek

Open your neglected heart and take a peek

At the boundless passion you have stored inside

To boost your own self-worth and individual pride

Instead of waiting on another outside entity

To provide you with your rightful God-given identity

To make you come to grips and finally see

What you as a God's creation should ultimately be

God wants us to be fruitful and multiply

But not in unhappiness and discontentment's cry

As a result that some relationships come to

Trying to make their earthy commitments stay true

You were born alone and will die alone

Most will forget you soon after you are gone

Realize that you can be alone and not be lonely

You will always have you and you only

Pro-speck-Tive

It always humbles me to think

We are merely just a speck of dust

Among a billion other specks of dust

Living on just a speck of dust (Our Planet)

Among a billion other specks of dust

Spinning at over 1,000 miles per hour

While orbiting just another speck of dust (Our Sun)

Among a billion other specks of dust

At approximately 66,000 miles per hour

These specks are constantly expanding and collapsing

Growing and dying at different rates of speed

From small specks to large specks

From large specks to small specks

Creating energy with each transformation

With each death or collapse heralding a new life

Each life or expansion promising a new death

All of this and more happens in the blink of God's eye

While these specks of dust are traveling through

The void of space at over 186,000 miles per second

Going to where we ain't got a clue of yet!!!

Put It In The Wind

Everyone has that thing they do

To help get through their day

Although from some, it comes ill-advised

I still prefer to do it my way

When I feel really pressured

To want to commit a deadly sin

I get on my Boom Trike motorcycle

And leave my troubles in the wind

Nothing relieves my life's problems

Like riding my trusty steed

Feeling the wind against my body

Accelerating at near breakneck speed

All too often we fall prey

To the webbed traps of our mind

Leaving us lost and susceptible

To give up on all mankind

These are the decisive moments

To take your motorcycle for a spin

Listen to some nice music

And leave your troubles in the wind

If everyone owned a motorcycle

Along with a truck or a car

There would be more love and respect

For motorcycles and their riders by far

Everyone would truly feel

How much stress you relieve to ride

Especially with friends and others

Riding along by your side

If you want to replace your doctors and pills

To relieve some of the funk you're in

Just get on your motorcycle

And simply "Put it in the Wind"

Q & A

For most of my life I wished

For something

I could not have at the time

My desires usually exceeded

My accomplishments

Of the present

The thirst for more and better

For the most part outweighed

The deeds of the past

Now I realize there is no end

Or finite achievement to life

It miraculously unfolds into a new death

Leading to a segue with each death

Culminating into the beginning of a new life

It is a vicious perpetual cycle

Of unresolved conclusions

That lead to nowhere

But where you began

With the same

Why, who, what, where questions

Concluding with the same

I know, I think so

I don't even care answers

Nobody really knows

And those who profess to know

Tell lies to themselves

They don't even know

That they don't know

Deluding their minds

With a false sense of reality

With promises of when I get there

What I am going to have

And who I am going to share it with

Footsteps

After traveling down life's arduous path

I hear footsteps behind me at last

Beckoning me to stop and wait

But for this reunion I have not set a date

I dare not dally or even miss a heart beat

For these footsteps would love to find my feet

Constantly chasing me to my inevitable end

In order for their new way of thinking to begin

These are the persistent footsteps of time

Waiting on me to come to a final grind

To cave in under life's relentless pace

But I refuse to give in to the chase

Of these annoying footsteps of time

Because I am fleet of foot and sound of mind

Time waits for no one is often said

But my objective keeps me one step ahead

Just one whole step is all I need

To outdistance the footsteps' constant pleas

For me to stop, look and turn around

Yet I still refuse to yield and bow down

To let the footsteps have their selfish way

For I have made plans for another day

Eventually they will catch up with me

After I fulfill my final manifest destiny

And I will have to cut a real deal

With them at last for my fate to seal

Only then will I bow down and take a knee

And allow the footsteps of time to set me free

Debbie Doo

(D.P.W.)

I wrote this just for you Debbie Doo

An all-knowing woman of wisdom who

If I had only listened earlier to

I'd still be able to dance the Boogaloo

Your concern was only for my life

When you first advised me to go under the knife

But I did not take heed to your advice

Because of lots of fear, stress and strife

Along with being utterly confused and vain

From ill advice from others and racked with pain

With utter feelings of no hope to remain

Coupled with signs of nothing left to gain

But to my good fortune and surprise

You finally made me open my eyes

For the surgery that I had to oblige

So that my body would not completely paralyze

When upon your insistence I set a date

For my doctor at last to operate

Then he said I was a bit too late

After surgery it would be difficult to ambulate

He also made it very clear and plain

That although I would be healthy and sane

And even have to walk with a cane

I will still have my wisdom and a good brain

Which at this point really matters first

Instead of having the situation in reverse

After all it could have been a lot worse

I could have wound up in the back of a hearse

So here's to you Debbie Doo

You changed my whole life's point of view

To make me do what I had to do

And for that I will always cherish you

Dear Weez

(A.K.A. Louise Williams)

I am very flattered

That what I write mattered

That you think I should recite

Live on an open mike

You speak of me being on spoken words

To express my poetic means

But I am very shy

Staying behind the scenes

It would be very nice

Knowing what you do

To express my writings

Coming from you

You have what people like

To be heard from an open mike

A voice worth listening to

That has a profound point of view

So I'd be honored for you to represent me

Giving all my glory to thee

For being very supportive and driven

For all of the praises you have given

Making you perfect to recite

The poetry to the public I write

No one else can relate

What I try to articulate

To be more clear

Than you Weez my dear

Living To Die For

(Inspired by Louise Williams A.K.A. Weez)

We all will eventually grow old if we just keep on living

That's a natural birthright not a choice that we were given

We knew not the infinite pleasures of life

Nor the unfathomable abyss of doom

As we entered this dark cold world

From our mother's warm womb

But yet here we are now

Struggling to stay afloat

Swimming in a sea of confusion

Without a paddle or a boat

Death is inescapable if we keep on living

Living is most fulfilling if we keep on giving

Never giving up to stop or just to be hanging

But like a monkey in a tree made to keep on swinging

Like a caterpillar with no wings born only to crawl

Before morphing into a beautiful butterfly

That simply refuses to fall

Life, like art, is never completed only halted and set aside

In order to gain momentum for another long stride

Sooner or later we will succumb

To the unyielding laws of earth's gravity

That beckons us back to our origin

Like the ebb tides of the sea

Where death is merely a temporary stay

To rest one's world-weary soul

For life to make a new transition

To embark on another goal

The whole process with its immense joys

And total anarchy of war

Makes it all quite unique

And worth living to die for

Pharmageddon

Have you ever thought about the drug epidemic today

And how it is being waged and controlled in a different way

Most people now fulfill their drug-induced fantasies

By shopping at their neighborhood pharmacies

Where all they need is a doctor's prescription

To get as high as they want to with no reservation

No more hiding and ducking from the cops

While scoring drugs from the local neighborhood stops

Big Pharma has this business monopolized

To ensure their drug is the only one people are supplied

They drug-test them before they get their prescription

Making sure that their drug is the only one in their system

And lo and behold if they ever want to go holistic

Big Pharma and the doctors will go ballistic

They want them on legal drugs like Oxycodone and Vicodin

That kill more people than marijuana, cocaine and heroin

If you don't believe me, then look it up

And read about this dangerous new legal stuff

This new drug epidemic isn't fueled by illegal street dealers

But instead by legalized pharmaceutical pill dispensers

Killing more people yearly by the multitudes and scores

Than any of the neighborhood drug-dealing doors

They keep people in a fog not knowing what's real

All from the effects of just a small legal pill

Today our biggest fear is not the coming of Armageddon

But the rapidly growing presence of Pharmageddon

Tomorrow

People ask me all of the time

What are you doing tomorrow

As if that is a sure day

For me to lend or borrow

From a time not promised to me

Unless my past allows it be

Excuse me if I sound a little dumb

But to some tomorrow will never come

Which is why you should cherish each day

That fate shines life your way

To make the most of today

As opposed to squirreling things away

Waiting for time to permit you to buy

Your own piece of pie in the sky

Your future is somewhat based on your past

Without a solid past, your future may not last

Even on a completely good day

Tomorrow can miraculously go away

When asked about plans for tomorrow

These simple words I must bestow

THE FIRST PLAN IS TO AWAKEN

THE REST OF MY PLANS ARE NOT TAKEN

We Still Rise

The LI Super Bowl has come and gone

With the Patriots as the victors occupying the throne

The strategy in this game brought my mind to bear

A classic example of the Tortoise and the Hare

With the Falcons taking off with "guns a blazing"

While the Patriots lay back in their hammock "just a lazing"

They knew the Falcons would soon run out of gas

And their big lead they started with would not last

Because they have been here nine times before

They knew just how and when to score

For the Falcons who are still in their prime

This makes it only their second time

Leaving them at a loss of how to expect

What the Patriots from experience might do next

Finally in O.T., the Pats put the Birds back in their cage

Then prepared for their role on center stage

As Champions of the LI Super Bowl Game

Placing them in the prestigious Hall of Fame

A place they have earned the right in which to be

Considering their outstanding football history

The Falcons did great I ain't even mad

But in the end the Patriots were just too bad

It's over for now but don't worry, fret or fear

We will be back for blood next year

With a team more agile, stronger and wise

Though this year we fell, next year we still rise

Once Again

Once again my lifestyle has been compromised

By unforeseen events that often arise

A promise of love has raised its fickle head

By another woman willing to share my bed

Willing to share my dark secrets and woes

With promises of things not to disclose

Of info not to be told or shared

Because of how much they cared

But in a breakup they will spread

All of your private info that you dread

To your friends and family near

And anyone with a listening ear

Making you the villain of the day

Why does it always have to end that way

It would be nice to have a never-ending love

Sanctioned by the almighty God above

One that would eventually outlast

The bumps and bruises of each other's past

But our past puts us in each other's headlights

For each of us to adjust and aim our sights

Focusing on each other's evil intent

To administer a more direct fatal hit

Based on issues of an unfounded consequence

Spawned by a suspicious blatant remiss

I don't think love was meant to be

Something to last for all eternity

I think it's merely a stepping-stone

To prepare you for being alone

To understand the infinite wealth

That lies within your own true self

To Bi Or Not To Bi

I grew up in the 1950s in a binary constructed era

When the consequence of being diverse was a real terror

A couple was always thought as being Adam and Eve

Not Mary and Eve or Adam and Steve

It was back then just not politically correct or society's way

To recognize an entity that was black, brown, yellow or gay

They never considered that the people that were deemed gay

Were like that because they were born that way

They would justify their prejudice and religious take

By them believing that "their" God never makes a mistake

And viewed everyone else as an abomination

If they were not Jewish, White or Aryan Nation

But in this new world of knowledge we now live in

It is not considered to be a deadly sin

To be what or whoever you want to be

Without losing your basic rights or human dignity

Today's consensus makes the binary construct a relic of
the past

With nonbinary gender constructs here to last

Although there are lots of choices of which I do not agree

That others make that do not concern me

People still have a right to act and voice

Their own opinions and God-given choice

About their individual points of reference

And their personal private sexual preference

If it doesn't directly interfere with what I am doing

It's not my business who other people are wooing

I am willing to accept all others' sex and gender

As long as my freedom of choice I don't have to surrender

From Peter To Paul

The "Feel Good" drugs that we created

Are a little bit overrated

The cure for what hurts and ails us

Also makes us crazy, crippled or kills us

We take pills to get a quick relief

Only to wind up with a much greater grief

What we do to make the pain pass

Usually comes back and bites us in the ass

The older you get, the more you ache

The more you ache, the more you take

The more you take, the more you need

The more you need, the less you take heed

To your dwindling desire for love and sex

And some other drug side effects

We haven't got the slightest clue at all

That we're just "Robbing Peter to pay Paul"

There's really no getting ahead

Until you're almost damn near dead

The bright future that you used to seek

Has become desolate and bleak

Sooner or later Peter will come back into view

To come collect what he's past due

So take all your "Feel Good" pills today

For tomorrow to Peter you will definitely pay

Trust

Trust is something that always seems to change

With the number of friends over time who remain

Still living who interact daily with you

While sharing a common point of view

In youth, your trust is wide open

To all your friends who seem well spoken

Who could sell an Eskimo, a block of ice

Just because they seem honest and nice

At midlife, your distrust of some friends becomes more

As their dependability becomes a swinging door

Allowing them access to your life to go in and out

Spreading misinformation about what you are about

More than likely they are jealous of your accomplishment

And hate the way their lives finally went

These are the friends who you do not need

If in life you want to prosper and succeed

Then with experience your trust become more olden

And your belief in friends becomes more golden

Allowing only a select few to infiltrate

Your trust's prized golden gate

These are the friends to trust with your life

To take heed to their worldly advice

That will help guide you through

The hidden paths that you are blind to

Cherish these friends till death do you part

Because they have your best interest at heart

Mother Nature's Dance

I open my windows in the spring

To let in the symphony that nature will bring

I open my doors to cast out

My mind's winter cobwebs and seeds to sprout

As new life arises from my cobwebs and seeds

Everything awakens to fulfill nature's needs

The stage is being set for Mother Nature's dance

In a season for all of God's creatures to romance

For them to go forth and choose their mate

To unite, propagate and perpetuate

Her dance's melody is sung by mocking birds

With robins and sparrows chirping its words

A woodpecker pecks a staccato drum

As windblown pine needles strum

As anyone with eyes and ears will testify

Nature's digital surround sound you can't deny

Her dance will last until late fall

When Mother Nature makes her last curtain call

For old man winter is coming soon

As sure as the setting sun and the rising moon

He brings a different dance to the stage

Of cold arctic blasts and winter rage

All of God's creatures slow to a creep

Before everything goes back to sleep

His dance will not last for very long

For Mother Nature's desires are headstrong

She's brimming over with life-giving pride

That just can't be ignored or denied

Spring is just around the bend

Then Mother Nature's dance starts over again

Coming Up In The A.T.L.

I was born in the early fifties in Atlanta's Thomasville Heights

I was as happy as a child could be with no major plights

I grew up on what I guess really could have been a farm

It was then part of the city that still possessed country charm

We had goats, chickens, cows, roosters and a few pigs

You could go outside in the backyard half-naked and pick figs

Thomasville had more to offer than most neighborhoods

On a nice day my dogs and I would go exploring in the woods

One favorite place for us was a pond full of tadpoles and frogs

Everything was so open that people rarely tied up their dogs

The dogs were free to chase rabbits and even a car someday

I often wondered what would they do with a car anyway

Being young I'd imagine the woods as an enchanted forest

With dinosaurs, dragons, deep valleys and hills like Mt. Everest

The woods had streams, little animals and plenty of colorful birds

It was a picture too beautiful to be expressed in mere words

In the fall, it strongly scented of scuppernongs and muscadines

The aromatic fragrance led you right to their fruit-laden vines

In the summer, there were plums, pears and strawberries

There were also pecans, walnuts, mulberries and wild cherries

Those nuts and fruits we ate for free are now sold as organic

They were naturally grown having the best taste on the planet

In Thomasville, there was never a stranger you'd meet

You'd never worry about having something to eat or drink

If you were at a friend's house while your parents were gone

Their parents would keep and feed you like one of their own

They also had the right to punish if you did something wrong

Then you'd get punished again when your parents got back home

Atlanta rose from a city of folks with chewing tobacco in their mouth

To a metropolis known as The International Hub of the South

I have never been to any faraway places like China, Paris or Rome

But if I had been, my choice would still be to make Atlanta my home

God's Gift

Everyone has a gift given to them by God

Even if you consider yourself a total retard

Some people race fast cars for a living

That is their gift God has given

Some can dance or figure skate

Some know how to sell real estate

God endowed everyone with a special skill

For you to use as you will

The trick is to learn it to use

Not to doubt it or abuse

For me I find writing not so hard

Because that is my gift from God

Writing requires a certain knack

That some have and others lack

Don't ever think that God has denied you

Your gift and what you are due

Often your gift is hidden behind life's doors

Maybe buried under life's floors

You have to be patient enough to know

Which door to enter and not to go

Or to dig up the floor or not

To find the right spot

The final choice is up to you

To do or not to do

God can give you water to drink

But he cannot make you think

So if you can't figure out your own worth

You will definitely die of thirst

"Family Upbringin"

In this life no one is exempt

From the world's evils that tempt

Us to cross over to the "dark" side

Bartering our souls against family pride

Life is replete with lots of temptation

That beckons you to hell's damnation

From sex, drugs and rock and roll

All of which takes a heavy toll

But you have to stay positive and strong

Be alert and keep on moving on

If you hit rock bottom, start back climbing to the top

Don't just lie around and flip-flop

I've had bouts with demons that made me wonder

Why I survived without being pulled under

The only thing that kept me from sinking

Was a positive family upbringing

My family has always been very strong

Teaching me what's right from wrong

If I started to straggle and stray

They showed me back to the right way

Family upbringing is the key to your survival

To cast out the demons before they become you

If you have good morals that you believe in

Give full credit to your "Family's Upbringin"

Love From Within

How can you get to love me

If you abhor what your eyes see

Making all of your decisions

Based upon skin colors and religions

How can you get to know me inside

Without swallowing your earthly pride

Which makes you rude and unkind

And socially people conscious blind

Trust me with your eyes

And I will return favor with mine

To see my true person as a whole

Look through your eyes into my soul

Only there can you seek to cast out

The dreaded illusive seeds of doubt

To learn it's not a carnal sin

To find love from within

Driving Me Insane

Early morning driving

Is all about surviving

Going to my day job

With the early morning mob

Running just a little late

Trying to keep food on my plate

Cutting in and out of lanes

Like a fool with no brains

Even the school bus is going fast

That you can't even pass

With kids fighting and cussing

While they are constantly bussing

Them across to another town

Cause their local school is shut down

You have to be a wee bit surly

To drive in the morning early

And you might get the finger

If at the light you linger

It's all about the dollar

That we all have to follow

Trying to be retired

Before we get fired

So keep on driving and stay strong

You will be off before too long

Then it's early evening driving

Still about surviving

That starts all over again

With no way to win

Driving in traffic has made me crazy

Leaving my brain a little hazy

It is now documented, clear and plain

DRIVING HAS DRIVEN ME INSANE

Happy New Day

The most celebrated time that people hold dear

Is one day called Happy New Year

What about the 364 days in between

Surely there is something that they mean

Shouldn't they be called happy too

After all they are also brand new

If you awaken to see a new sunrise

Against the backdrop of new blue skies

Some people whose times are growing near

Might not survive to see another new year

Why do we have to gamble and wait

A whole year just to celebrate

I have a new slogan that I want to say

Instead of Happy New Year, it's

HAPPY NEW DAY

Entertainer's Lament

Hi I am your host for the evening

Always able, willing and pleasing

To provide you some distractions

From your worldly infractions

I am your puppet on a string

That can act, dance and sing

To the point of my abasement

Just for your amusement

Nobody concerns about my life

About my aches, pains and strife

Nobody cares about my monthly bills

As long as I provide pleasures and thrills

Does anybody really care

About what I eat and wear

They only see what they want me to be

Because I am a mere celebrity

Just performing on a stage

To ease their daily rage

But nobody knows who I am

And don't even give a damn

So I just keep doing what I do

For a select audience to view

Even though parts of my skits

To some might not be big hits

At the risk of being insane

I'm still willing to entertain

Female Math

There is a new math that women use

That they are starting to openly abuse

To hold men under their little thumb

While keeping their brains confused and numb

Actually it is very old and not at all new

Because Eve used this math on Adam too

When she gave him the forbidden fruit to bite

Assuring him that things would be all right

It was designed to keep men in self-doubt

Preventing them from running all about

While I must admit some men ain't too bright

We still know what's wrong from what's right

Women add things up differently and some men never see

How and why they make one and one equal three

Then when they think they might get caught in a little lie

Their addition and subtraction start to multiply

They make three times ten equal seventy-seven

And eighty times ninety-nine come out to eleven

Female math is as old as the universe

And most men still don't know why it works

I think this math works on most of us

Because of our undying love and trust

We have for our family-oriented women

That keeps our head spinning and swimming

Making it forgivable and not a deadly sin

If they fudge the numbers every now and then

As long as we both are happy and satisfied

Men should take female math in stride

Stature Or Status???

Why is it that most women want to meet

A man who is a little taller than six feet

Leaving shorter men with a Napoleon Complex

When trying to deal with the opposite sex

Not even providing a shorter man a fighting chance

To form an everlasting loving romance

Even women no taller than four foot eleven

Want a man about six foot seven

Giving shorter men enough inferior complexes

To stretch from here to West Texas

Women will bypass a true-blue five-foot-five Eddy

And take up with a six-foot-three lie-slinging Freddy

Maybe they just want a man to look up to

Not across, sideways or down to

Maybe they want to be able to climb on his back

Then ride him like a wild Tibetan yak

Then maybe it's inherent in their DNA

And they were just born that way

Whatever the real reason is

It causes shorter men lots of tears

To be rejected for not being born to be tall

And not being able to dunk a fricking basketball

Women need to wake up and reevaluate

That being tall don't pay for their dinner plate

Judge not by the height of one's physical stature

But instead the accomplishments from their social status

If some women process this in their already made-up mind

They might learn that a short man is sometimes good to find

I.C.U.
(I SEE YOU)

COVID COVID where are you??

When when is my time due??

For you to finally catch up with me

I guess I will just have to wait and see

Will you catch me at Wally World purchasing my Cheerios

Or riding my Trike in the wide open outdoors

In the doctor's office that should be safe and secure

At this moment I don't think nobody's really sure

Maybe at the local market buying my fruits and nuts

I am so confused now I don't know who to trust

It seems to be inevitable that COVID is out to get us all

Before the season change this upcoming fall

There is lots of misinformation on why and how COVID is spread

But they really won't know until you are cold and dead

Some say it's a government plot to "thin the herd"

And "voila" the population decreases without a mumbling word

No more reason to wage wars to do it

Having a virus is more humane and fluid

Some say it's Mother Nature's way to protect herself

By ridding the earth of humans for her own future and health

Apparently dinosaurs must have also disagreed with her view

Because after millions of years, she finally got rid of them too

Either way it seems to be working right on plan

Right now things look kind of bleak for the future of man

Proactive Or Reactive

If we could take today's experiences into tomorrow

There would be less pain and sorrow

If we could implement our future plans

Based upon today's supplies and demands

We would be one step ahead

With no fears and worries to dread

But we are programmed to learn on the go

The future knowledge we will never learn to know

The past and present we are shown

But the future is in the forbidden zone

We live in a "I want it now" situation

With a "Not caring about tomorrow" fixation

A "Cross that bridge when you come to it" species

That comes, goes and does what it damn well please

Maybe we are afraid of what's to come

So we cling to where we come from

Then avoid making lengthy future plans

By hiding our heads like an ostrich in the sands

One day maybe we will learn to be proactive

Instead of being past and present reactive

Then start making future upcoming decisions

Based on our past innermost visions

The Big Show

OK....READY ON THE SET......CAMERA.......ACTION

Welcome to the stage, welcome to the show

Come on in and tell us what you know

About where you live and what you ate

And where you went on your last dinner date

Every day we awaken to perform on the stage

To display our simple pleasures and unbridled rage

To anyone with a bending ear to hear

Some of the things we hold true and dear

Thanks to social medias and the information highway

We all perform on the stage every single day

We take selfies and videos to post on Facebook

Then monitor how many people "like" the look

With an utter complete blind obedience

To a sometimes unknown audience to view us

We get our ratings for performing on the stage

Without rehearsing or reading a single script or page

We get high ratings for the stellar performance we gave

That made our worst critics awe and rave

Low ratings for our ignorance and stupidity

Meant to rob us of the last of our dignity

We act in this show to seek approval from others

As if they were our fathers and mothers

To justify our role of showing hope for humanity

But it's only to check and stifle our own insecurity

We all are just actors in life's big show

Being broadcast live daily door to door

CUT......OK....THAT'S A WRAP

(Dropping my pen like rappers drop a mike)

Life's Mountains

Life is like an endless chain of mountain ranges

Replete with valleys and hills to scale

Sometimes you become lost going in circles

Like a dog chasing its own tail

Just when you think you've caught it

It becomes suddenly unreachable

Giving you one of life's lessons

That is totally unteachable

Some days you're deep down in the valley low

Other days on the mountain top high

Some days everything is dark and dreary

Other days sunny with blue sky

Just when you make it to the top

There's another valley to descend

Leading to another mountain

Of which you are to begin

Life's mountain climbing is very hard

You will not make it to the top in one day

So stop and rest your weary feet

And have fun along the way

What makes life's mountain climbing great

Is the fantastic unseen view from each top

So as long as you are able

Keep climbing and never never stop

Staying Clean In 2016

(J.R.'s Pledge)

I don't care what everyone drinks

I don't care what everyone eats

I don't care about what others do

Their sexual proclivities or their party treat

If they want to go jump off a cliff

Sniff powder that makes them sneeze

As long as they don't put it in my nose

They can very well do as they please

If they want to take a few pills

Roll up a "fatty" and smoke a little weed

I could really care less

If that's what they feel they need

As for me I'm too old for dumb stuff to be trying

While some are my friends around me are dying

If you keep on doing drugs

Sooner or later it will take its toll

Then you will end up like them

Six feet deep in a hole

I have already experienced death once

I don't want to do it again

The book that I read

States that suicide is a sin

If you keep on doing drugs

You are just killing yourself

If you don't die right away

You may end up with bad health

Sometimes dealing with life ain't no joke

But I've come too far to see it go up in smoke

That's why I'm keeping my mental focus keen

To stay clean in 2016

Dad

(01/05/1912–11/24/1992)

In nineteen twelve, Nazareth Knox was born

Into a world of discrimination and scorn

He grew up when times were extremely hard

To hustle with a skill was considered very smart

He quit high school when he was about fifteen

To seek what life's school had for him to glean

He learned that sometimes book knowledge makes you dumb

But street knowledge and a skill can always be relied upon

"Hit ain't no book on life," he often said

"Regardless of what kinds of books you have read"

Therefore, armed with ambition and an eighth-grade education

He decided to become a plasterer and cement mason

Although jobs and opportunities in life were few

He managed to work and fight his way through

Dad was a jack-of-all-trades and a master of none

He would not quit until the job was done

Dad made sure that all of his children developed a skill

He knew that a skill would always provide a good meal

Dad helped to raise eleven children and gave his best

Even though some of us did put him to the test

Growing up we often did not see eye to eye

When I had a son, I quickly found out why

It takes a lot of patience to raise a son

Life is not always about games and fun

Often you have to give a son tough love

For him to see life's pitfalls and rise above

We all adhered to the lessons our dad taught

We learned that life is not always without fault

All eleven of his children have his great gift

We are all mentally adroit, agile and swift

Dad passed away peacefully at almost eighty-one years old

Assured that his legacy's roots had firmly taken hold

Mom

(10/05/1913–01/09/2010)

When she was born back in nineteen thirteen

God blessed her with the makings of a queen

A woman of color with such moral convictions

That she had no desires for mere worldly addictions

A woman brimming over with honor and pride

She was basically fearless with nothing to hide

Although at times she could be extremely vain

At ninety-six she still refused to use a cane

She said it made her look crippled and old

And to look crippled and old was not her goal

This woman fed and clothed a crew of eleven

While always keeping her vows to God and heaven

She was always at home when I arrived from school

With a hot meal, good cheer and the golden rule

If you misbehaved, the rule would be on your behind

Then you got sent to bed without a chance to dine

When I had kids, that same rule I did apply

For them to grow up honest and not lie

I remember when I was only about three or four

She caught me under the house with the little girl next door

She literally whipped the skin off of both of us

As we "danced" around in all of the dirt and dust

Then she said "this hurt me more than it hurt you"

At three or four I did not find that to be true

After the little girl ran home across the street

Never again in life did our eyes meet

When mom was done and everything was through

At once a valuable lesson of life came into view

My brothers and sisters still tease me up to this day

They still just will not let a sleeping dog lay

After that I listened to her words of wit

There's no way I wanted any more of that S _ _ T

Then my mom and I developed a special bond

And I am proud and honored to be her son

My Idols

I was born the tenth child out of eleven

Giving me a type of spoiled heaven

That protected me from harm's way

From my birth right up until today

Being born as the baby boy

Was as much a curse as it was a joy

With four brothers and six sisters on "standby"

That no one would not even think to try

I knew no one would bother me

Fearing reprisals that might come to be

From them assaulting their baby brother

A storm they could not weather

So I never had to fuss and fight

Even if I was deemed wrong or right

They were always right by my side

Enforcing the time-honored "Knox Pride"

They were all technical and college-educated

And "in the hood street knowledge"-rated

Providing them an understanding that came to be

What they eventually bestowed upon me

When asked who influenced my life the most

My brothers and sisters deserve the biggest toast

Unlike giving praise to people I don't know

Like Obama, Oprah and Rapper Fat Joe

I chose idols who really knew me

And what I could potentially come to be

Making me into the man I am today

Because of their nurturing, loving, guiding way

Lessie's Report

It all happened on January ninth two thousand and ten

Lessie Knox was united back with Nat Knox Sr. again

They had parted on November twenty-fourth nineteen ninety two

When Nat Knox's date with God and heaven was due

Now they are finally back together at last

So she can update him on the things that have gone past

This is how I imagine the conversation might sound

"Nat, lots of things have happened since you've not been around

Our kids and grandkids don't have a whole lot of bad habits

Except lately they have started multiplying like Jack Rabbits

Between November 24th, 1992, and the present

We've got enough grands and great-grands to span the desert

It seems like they just started coming from everywhere

Every time I look around there was another one there

But I learned the more the merrier was really true

Because I love all of them, from the oldest to the new

I love each one of them in their own special way

I called and sang to each one of them on their birthday

None of them turned out to be famous, rich or wealthy

But they are fine kids honest, loyal and healthy

From Sylvia our very first child born out of eleven

To Kelsey D. our great granddaughter from heaven

We can be proud of each and every one

Now we can rest because our job is done"

Yah Mon, Respect

Yah Mon, Respect is what they say

As Jamaica awakens every day

From her nighttime slumber naps

Just like her native feral cats

First she yawns, then she stretches

Spreading her allure from here to Texas

Now it's time for her to prowl and feed

Feasting upon only what she needs

Taking no more than what it requires

For the survival of her people's desires

Like the feral cat you feed but cannot pet

Always staying an arm's length away

You enjoy them for the moment

Even if they will never stay

Because you can never own her

She's made for all to share

From the filthy, filthy rich

To the poor on welfare

Jamaica belongs on center stage

And on this I think everyone would bet

The prettiest sight you will ever see

Is a lovely Jamaican sunset

"IRIE MON"

Jammed In Jamaica

I am jammed in Jamaica

Because of Irma the hurricane

But thanks to the local "Med Doc"

I am feeling no pain

I am at the Grand Palladium Resort

In Lucea by Montego Bay

Surrounded by bathing suit-clad beauties

With long legs forever and a day

I met a very nice lady

By the name of Angelene

Who talked to me to ease my tension

She is truly a Jamaican Queen

The weather is pleasant and fine

The music is fantastic and great

I could nourish a small country

With how much I drank and ate

The night ocean breeze is refreshing

The evening sunset is spectacular

And, YAH MON, I even learned

A little Jamaican vernacular

Still I will be so happy when

Irma gives us a little reprieve

Turn the wind down just a bit

So that I can pack up and leave

Jammed in Jamaica

And I am ready to go home

I really love Jamaica

But Atlanta, GA, is where I belong

"IRIE MON"

Gravity

As I slowly yield to gravity

With all of its humility

I am finding some serenity

In my new-found senility

Realizing that what it takes to grow old

Ain't to be talked about or told

But learned by living and doing

Your life's dreams you are pursuing

Growing old is not for the weak, but for the strong

Without being strong you won't last too long

No one gets to where they are going

Without some forethought or knowing

That life is not always simple and fair

Akin to trying to split a fine hair

When in life there's nothing else to gain

You will go the bottom of the food chain

Where gravity starts to make haste

Leaving nothing lost or going to waste

The process may seem cruel and destructive

But the end result is humane and productive

Sooner or later gravity will win

Beckoning you back to where you begin

Back to the Mother Earth that birth you

Back to the gracious God who made you

Dichotomy Of A Species

When we say, "I don't know if I'm coming or going"

It holds true without us thinking about or knowing

Man as a species has a very serious dual personality

That either clarifies, destroys or distorts our reality

Some species of animals have tusks and thick hides

Our species has thin skin and a brain with two sides

One side seeks wealth, longevity and the good life

It wants perfection, simplicity and no strife

The other side has a morbid penchant for death

It craves for failure, diseases and bad health

We attend church and praise God all day on Sunday

Then commit blasphemy and cuss all day on Monday

We smoke cigars and cigarettes and drink to our demise

The next morning when we arise, we jog and exercise

The brain is split equally on both sides, yes indeed

One to satisfy our want, the other to fulfill our need

One side promises to go straight and never sin again

The other side can hardly wait for sin to kick in

Man has a unique, uncanny built-in defeatist attitude

Coupled with a highly intense desire to win mood

We thrive for wealth, success, love and fame

Then we make plans to fall short of our aim

We try to please everybody but not ourselves

While our own dreams lie dormant on the shelves

Maybe in the future the huge gap between the two

Will bridge itself and the brain will be made anew

Then maybe it would not flip and flounder around

This would make our species' judgment more profound

DANA

I woke up this morning

In a brand-new world

Because "DANA" told me yesterday

I have a new baby girl

One born fully clothed with teeth

And already walking

She came in on a motorcycle

Card playing and smack talking

There is no doubt she's mine

I can always tell

By the way she acts

And that new baby smell

"DANA" said I have three grandsons

Who I didn't know I had

Already potty-trained

For that I ain't even mad

When "DANA" speaks

You have to stop and listen

Or else some of your past

You will be missing

I have to accept this as truth

Because that's what "DANA" say

Who also goes by another name

called D.N.A.

True First Love

Fifty years ago I met the first love of my life

Who I should have made my beautiful wife

We were very young and deeply in love

Sanctioned by the angels and God from above

She was as lovely as lovely could be

No maiden in the land more fairer than thee

Her voice was soft like a summer breeze

Whistling through tall pine needle trees

I was sure our love would last forever and a day

Nothing could keep our first love from having its way

After a year and eight months, we unexpectedly parted

Leaving us both sad and broken-hearted

Wondering what if or what could have been

And was this love really God-sent

Recently I just got back in touch with her

Only to find out that I still do love her

Will fate allow me to atone from the past???

Is true first love meant to last???

We can only see where it goes

In the end only God above knows

If true first love really conquers all

Or you're just headed for the next fall

Whichever way it goes I'll gladly take a chance

If it could lead to another first-love romance

Majul

Majul "My Jewel" where have you been

Why did God wait so long to send

You through the rains of my tears

Over four decades and eight years

For you to finally find a way to see

Your way home back to me

In my heart I felt you being there

But I just did not know where

You are a rare gem, a precious jewel

You are truly my God's gift named Majul

That lights up the universe so bright

Like a supernova in the night

A light emerging from the past

Through the darkness here at last

Defying all the odds to become

Where you originated from

To find your rightfully due place

Amongst this vile unjust human race

Where you fit like a silk glove

Woven out of truth and pure love

Now that you are finally home

You will never again be alone

You can always depend on me

And the entire Knox Klan Family

Sixty-Six

At sixty-six I finally got smart

I found someone to trust with my heart

Who would not tear it into little pieces

Then devour it like chocolate-covered Reese's

Someone to share with my lifelong dream

And play as one on the same team

I also stopped drugging and drinking

What the hell was I thinking

That maybe I could drown out the past

With a stiff drink and a blast

Now I know that I have too much to lose

By smoking weed and drinking booze

As you get older, things rearrange

Which should precipitate a major change

To steer you in a whole new direction

For your own self-preservation

All of my life I have been told

If you live long enough, you will get old

There is one thing that just goes to show

What young folks ain't old enough to know

WHEN LIFE DEALS YOU ENOUGH HARD LICKS

YOU "CAN" TEACH AN OLD DOG NEW TRICKS

At sixty-six I finally got smart enough to see

The one to trust with my heart is me

Good Neighbors, Bad Knees

(To Chawn, Diane and George)

Thank God for good neighbors with good knees

Who can come and go as they please

Who always lend me a helping hand

Like bringing my mail and taking out my trash can

I tried to do these chores but my knees said don't

I asked my knees to walk but they just won't

Bad knees makes doing easy chores hard

Like bringing in the groceries and mowing the yard

Bad knees don't like to stand, they like to sit

Which makes sitting and watching TV an easy fit

They keep you from doing lots of things that you like

Hell I can't even ride my doggone Trike

So thank God for good neighbors with good knees

Who can still do their chores with ease

There is no amount I could ever pay you

For all of the things for me that you do

It's a blessing to live around such good neighbors

Who don't mind doing each other favors

If there's anything I can do for you with bad knees

Don't ever hesitate to ask me please

As long as the chore is aptly fitting

That I can do not standing but sitting

En Garde Ennui

Ennui don't darken my door today

For I have plans to be happy and play

I want to go shopping in the mall

Where there is no room for you at all

I want to go riding on my Trike

So ennui just go take a hike

I have lots of things I have to do

That does not include the likes of you

Sometimes you are good to have around

When I need to rest and settle down

But most of the time you're a pain in the azz

And I am so glad to see you pass

Ennui please don't start to pout

My mind is made up without a doubt

I'm sick and tired of you ruining my day

By running all of my joys away

Maybe you can come back after the holiday

Somewhere between April and May

Or better, give me a lifetime break

And simply just go jump in a lake

Whatever you do, just do it quick

Before the arrival of Rudolph and St. Nick

Whether you go by boredom or ennui

Today you just can't hang with me

America's Lawlessness

As I lay my head down to rest

Confident that I have passed the test

God have given me one more night

To arise in the morning and make it right

To amend some of these humanly flaws

That contradict his commands and laws

Although he did provide us with free will

It's still against his law to discriminate and kill

Based upon the color of a person's skin

And the kind of car that he was in

Like the people, we pay for our protection

Who view us as God's abomination

Now another precious life is gone

Because the driver just only had a cell phone

Instead of the nonexistent gun they visualized

In their written report of blatant lies

Which earns them a well-paid vacation

For killing someone over a minor traffic violation

Laws in America have never been right

All of our history we have had to fight

For freedom that should have been free

From the time we were brought from over the sea

They just passed a law allowing us to wear

In public our God-given beautiful hair

That grows naturally curly from our head

Which they wanted us to straighten instead

When will America wake up and see

Us all as Americans and set us free